ARCHITECTURAL DESIGN

GUEST-EDITED BY
TERRI PETERS

EXPERIMENTAL GREEN STRATEGIES
REDEFINING ECOLOGICAL DESIGN RESEARCH

06|2011

ARCHITECTURAL DESIGN
NOVEMBER/DECEMBER 2011
ISSN 0003-8504

PROFILE NO 214
ISBN 978-0470-689790
SPECIAL AUTODESK EDITION
ISBN 978-1119-967903

wiley.com

ARCHITECTURAL DESIGN

GUEST-EDITED BY
TERRI PETERS

EXPERIMENTAL GREEN STRATEGIES
REDEFINING ECOLOGICAL DESIGN RESEARCH

62

*Designing with concern for the
environment is a fundamental part
of architecture.* — *Terri Peters*

82

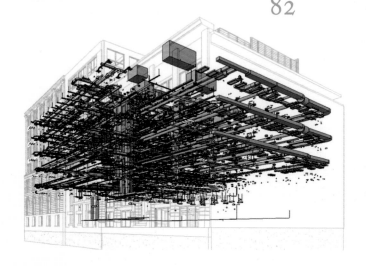

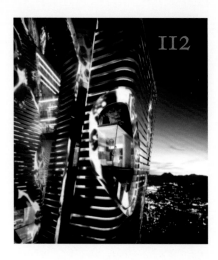

112

ARCHITECTURAL DESIGN
NOVEMBER/DECEMBER 2011
PROFILE NO 214

Editorial Offices
John Wiley & Sons
25 John Street
London
WC1N 2BS

T: +44 (0)20 8326 3800

Editor
Helen Castle

Managing Editor (Freelance)
Caroline Ellerby

Production Editor
Elizabeth Gongde

Prepress
Artmedia, London

Art Direction and Design
CHK Design:
Christian Küsters
Sophie Troppmair
Maryrose Simpson

Printed in Italy by Conti Tipocolor

Sponsorship/advertising
Faith Pidduck/Wayne Frost
T: +44 (0)1243 770254
E: fpidduck@wiley.co.uk

Subscribe to ⊿D

⊿D is published bimonthly and is
available to purchase on both a
subscription basis and as individual
volumes at the following prices.

Prices
Individual copies: £22.99 / US$45
Mailing fees may apply

Annual Subscription Rates
Student: £75 / US$117 print only
Individual: £120 / US$189 print only
Institutional: £200 / US$375 print or
online
Institutional: £230 / US$431 combined
print and online

Subscription Offices UK
John Wiley & Sons Ltd
Journals Administration Department
1 Oldlands Way, Bognor Regis
West Sussex, PO22 9SA
T: +44 (0)1243 843272
F: +44 (0)1243 843232
E: cs-journals@wiley.co.uk

Print ISSN: 0003-8504;
Online ISSN: 1554-2769

Prices are for six issues and include
postage and handling charges.
Individual rate subscriptions must be
paid by personal cheque or credit card.
Individual rate subscriptions may not
be resold or used as library copies.

All prices are subject to change
without notice.

Rights and Permissions
Requests to the Publisher should be
addressed to:
Permissions Department
John Wiley & Sons Ltd
The Atrium
Southern Gate
Chichester
West Sussex PO19 8SQ
England

F: +44 (0)1243 770620
E: permreq@wiley.co.uk

Front cover: Autodesk Research, Nested Flow, 2011.
© Duncan Brinsmead & Azam Khan
Inside front cover: Detail of Foster + Partners,
Specialist Modelling Group Focus and Activities,
2011. © Foster + Partners

EDITORIAL
Helen Castle

Just at the point that 'green' and 'sustainable' have become so ubiquitous as terms that they have come to mean nothing and everything to everyone, Guest-editor Terri Peters has produced an issue of ⌀ that reminds us of the real possibilities and relevance of the ecological. From the earliest point in our discussions, Terri and I were both convinced that in order to break new ground, this ⌀ had to focus on research. As she points out in her introduction, architecture continues to struggle as a discipline with the principles of academic research and the unguarded dissemination of professional knowledge. What she has, however, revealed here is a rich seam of practices internationally working in this area, willing to invest time communicating their ideas. This includes participation from large firms, such as Aedas, BNIM, Foster + Partners, HOK, Nikken Sekkei, Perkins+Will Canada (P+W) and 3XN, which have dedicated in-house research units; as well as architects Hoberman Associates and engineers Buro Happold, who collaborate together on the Adaptive Building Initiative (ABI); and smaller offices such as 2012Architecten, RAU Architects and 10 Design, which have chosen to more exclusively concentrate on this field, often joining forces with external specialists and research bodies. This is not to overlook the significant contributions to the discipline from other essential members of the design team, such as software developers, like Robert Aish, Azam Khan and Andrew Marsh at Autodesk, and multidisciplinary engineers Atelier 10.

Within this issue, a paradigm shift in priorities and profile is conspicuously apparent. Gone is the timber-clad idealism that was prevalent among sustainable advocates even a decade or so ago. It is no longer about aesthetics or just materials. This is a serious field, tackling pressing and complex issues, while navigating difficult guidelines and legislation. It also requires designers who bring a different set of skills to the table. Computer modelling and simulation have become fundamental to the field. It is notable that environmental design and computation have become conjoined, often sitting within the same research units in bigger practices. Smaller practices are no less savvy. Rotterdam practice 2012Architecten has an overarching onus on recycling; its tools of choice for both analysing and communicating ecological design are harvest maps, urban metabolism studies, material flow analysis and Sankey diagrams. Process has become king over form. Biomimicry that has so often previously been understood to be about directly imitating natural form, here is reinterpreted as the emulation of the performance of natural systems (see pp 44–7 and 48–53). The message could never be clearer than when Simos Yannas, Director of the Environment & Energy Studies Programme at the Architectural Association (AA), states in his opening sentence: 'Ecological should be understood here as referring to processes and outcomes that are sustainable.' ⌀

Sample pages from a selection of recent texts authored by Terri Peters in *Mark* magazine featuring architects and designers (left to right): Jenny Sabin, Chuck Hoberman, Philip Beesley, Stefan Forster, R&Sie, Ruairi Glynn, Philipp Schaerer, Mark Burry, Moritz Waldemeyer, Marc Fornes, Daniel Rybakken, Mette Ramsgard Thomsen, Beat Karrer, Trust in Design and 3xN.

Terri Peters is an architect, writer and researcher whose work maps new trajectories of ecological design through contemporary practice, academic research and pop culture. She has a global perspective, having lived and worked in Vancouver, Tokyo, Paris and then London, which was her adopted home for eight years. Since 2009 she has been based in Copenhagen.

Her practice of architecture involves critical investigation and reflection from multiple angles. She has a research degree in architectural history, has written more than 200 articles for specialist architecture and design magazines, and has worked as an architect in both small and large offices in the UK. She is currently a writer, instructor and PhD Fellow at Aarhus Arkitektskolen in Denmark.

Her work is formed around proposing ways that architects can engage with issues beyond conventional practice, exploring the integration of architecture with aspects of art, biology, computation, design and fashion. Recent work has contextualised the work of architects using biological systems, the potentials of responsive and adaptive building components, and the ways that computation and robotics are changing the way buildings are designed and built.

Peters' work explores how experimental architecture can infiltrate the current practice of sustainable design through alternative ways of measuring, representing, communicating, adapting and designing ecological buildings. It resists the notion that these approaches must be standardised and replicable, and proposes instead that multidisciplinary research is needed to bridge academia and professional practice and that seemingly alternative architectural approaches such as building renovation should take a central role in the future of ecological buildings and cities. Her PhD dissertation proposes a new design methodology for the sustainable transformation of modern housing through the analysis of radical strategies of reuse, ecology and inhabitation.

With this title of Δ, Peters defines and examines an emerging trend in contemporary architectural practices relating to the formation of sustainable design research groups. These research groups mark a shift in how environmental design is approached in practice, and how ecological research is coming to be valued within the profession. Δ

SPOTLIGHT

Computer simulation, modelling and diagrams are all key for the analysis of green strategies. Once developed, the effective presentation of this data and research is vital in order to convince clients and user groups of an experimental approach. This is exemplified by the work of Foster + Partners Specialist Modelling Group at Masdar and these captivating oculi views they created to map the sun's path.

WORM Rotterdam Harvest Map, 2010
The harvest map illustrates the regional sourcing of building materials for the WORM cultural platform in and around Rotterdam. WORM was constructed in 2005 and opened 2006.

● Delft

● Blankenberge, België

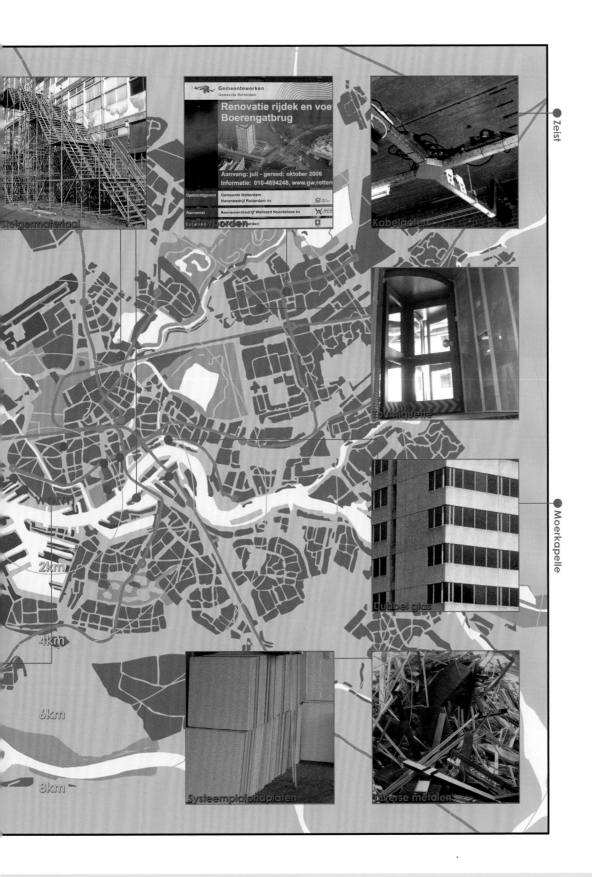

Steigermateriaal

Gemeentewerken
Gemeente Rotterdam

Renovatie rijdek en voe
Boerengatbrug

Aanvang: juli - gereed: oktober 2006
Informatie: 010-4894248, www.gw.rotterd

Opdrachtgevers Gemeente Rotterdam
Havenbedrijf Rotterdam nv

Aannemer Aannemersbedrijf Wallaard Noordeloos bv

bouwborden

Kabelgoten

Zeist

Tourniquette

Dubbel glas

Moerkapelle

2km

4km

6km

8km

Systeemplafondplaten

Diverse metalen

VanDusen Botanical Garden Visitor Centre,
Vancouver, 2011
Roof petals around the visitor centre oculus
establish the building's form.

*The visitor centre was the first project on which the P+W team
collaborated with an ecologist to inform the design of both
the building and the systems that affect its energy, water and
environmental performance. Ecologists look beyond property
lines to how plants and animals interact with the building and
surrounding ecosystem services.*

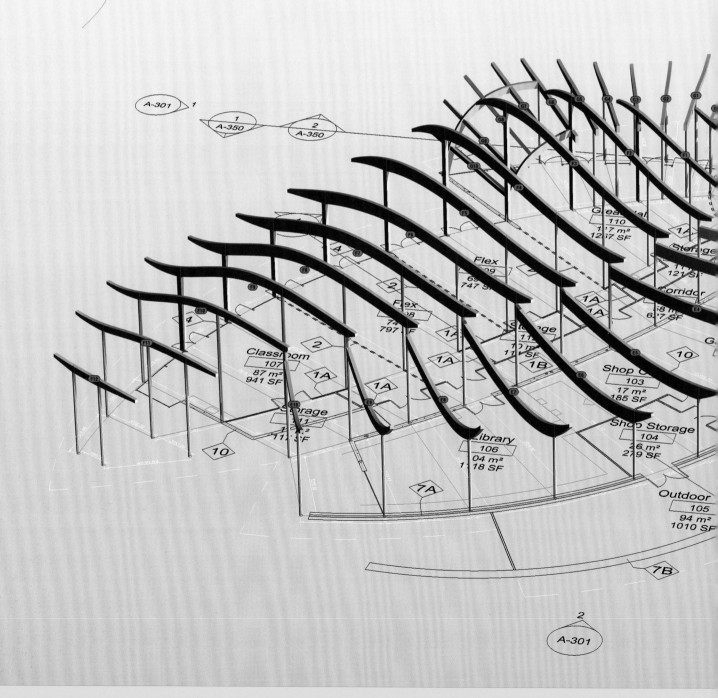

EXPERIMENTAL GREEN STRATEGIES

REDEFINING ECOLOGICAL DESIGN RESEARCH

Defining new ways in which architects are responding to the challenge of creating sustainable architecture, *Experimental Green Strategies* presents a state of the art in applied ecological, architectural research. But can a building be 'ecological'? How can architects in practice carry out 'research'? Is 'green' building a designer's problem, or does it depend on an ecology of building – enlightened clients, a new organisation of building practice and engaged users to participate in 'green strategies'?

This title of △ explores the way that pioneering designers are advancing sustainable architectural design, how contemporary practices are understanding the emerging brief of 'sustainability', and what sorts of new design tools and design approaches are being developed.

Approaching Ecological Building

Almost all architects except landscape architects have been trained without any serious background in ecology or environmental biology.[1] In his article 'What is Ecological Design?' in *The Green Skyscraper*, Ken Yeang suggests that what we are doing now as a profession is not ecological architecture, and that ecological design calls for a rapid and fundamental reorientation of our thinking and design approach with regard to the creation of our built environment.[2]

There are various ways to understand and define ecological architecture, and in this context it is necessary to consider architecture beyond buildings. Aaron Betsky's definition of architecture encompasses all of the things around building: 'Architecture is everything that is about building. It is how we think about building, how we draw buildings, how we organize buildings, how buildings present themselves … buildings are buildings; architecture is something different.'[3]

In his book *The Technology of Ecological Building*, engineer Klaus Daniels outlines principles for ecological building which include the need for a variety of detailed site studies, building form and orientation analysis, and local climate considerations.[4] His approach is concerned with optimisation, integration of building systems, and combining technological solutions with passive systems to improve performance. Daniels argues that buildings of the future should utilise state-of the-art materials and technologies in order to minimise energy demand and thus actively protect the environment.[5]

Architect and theorist Michael Lauring argues that the term 'ecological architecture' is loaded with cultural meaning, it changes over time and there is no clear definition. He believes the term was and is free for use. In a recent article in the *Nordic Journal of Architectural Research,* he explains: 'Slowly during the seventies "ecological" evolved from being a scientific, descriptive term to being a normative one, without any norm-criteria, but with lots of images and associations mostly of a rural kind.'[6] This issue of △ asks: How can ecological design be redefined towards a more relevant and architectural approach?

Foster + Partners Specialist Modelling Group, London, 2011
The Specialist Modelling Group (SMG) is an in-house consultancy at Foster + Partners, established in 1997 by Hugh Whitehead. It has continually fostered expertise in complex geometry, computer programming, parametric design, rapid prototyping and environmental simulation, contributing to more than a hundred of the firm's projects including the Swiss Re Headquarters, the Sage Gateshead Music Centre, London City Hall and the new Beijing International Airport.

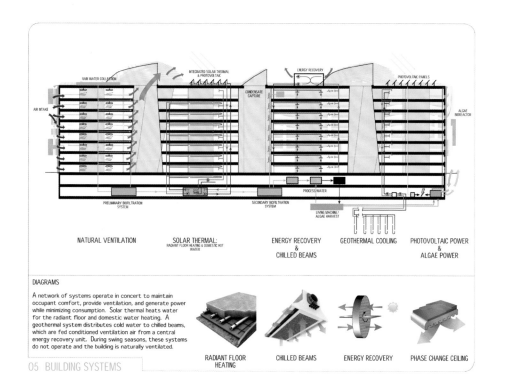

NATURAL VENTILATION SOLAR THERMAL: RADIANT FLOOR HEATING & DOMESTIC HOT WATER ENERGY RECOVERY & CHILLED BEAMS GEOTHERMAL COOLING PHOTOVOLTAIC POWER & ALGAE POWER

DIAGRAMS

A network of systems operate in concert to maintain occupant comfort, provide ventilation, and generate power while minimizing consumption. Solar thermal heats water for the radiant floor and domestic water heating. A geothermal system distributes cold water to chilled beams, which are fed conditioned ventilation air from a central energy recovery unit. During swing seasons, these systems do not operate and the building is naturally ventilated.

RADIANT FLOOR HEATING CHILLED BEAMS ENERGY RECOVERY PHASE CHANGE CEILING

Architects are looking outside the profession to allied fields in order to make sense of ecological design. Biomimicry expert and building consultant Janine Benyus (see 'Nature as Measure: The Biomimicry Guild', pp 44–7) defines ecological design as place-based, taking into consideration a site's unique ecology and specific land type. For Benyus, ecological design must take into consideration aspects of the site at differing scales, from the biological level to material and components, as well as at the scale of landscape and urbanism. Her hyperlocal approach insists on unique place-based solutions tailored to individual site and ecological needs. Where there are local needs there are local experts, and as Kevin Kelly argues in *Out of Control*, flows of information, materials and energy are complex and ever-changing as technology directs innovation towards the biological.[7] This relates in many ways to the definition by educator, architect and author Simos Yannas. In 'Adaptive Strategies for an Ecological Architecture' (see pp 62–9, Yannas argues that as currently conceived and practised, architecture neither is, nor is meant to be, ecologically sustainable: 'Making architecture ecologically sustainable will require its inanimate materiality to become attuned to the variable biological clocks and activities of occupants inside, and to similarly variable natural rhythms and mundane activities outside.' He suggests that architecture, like ecologies, must be considered over time, and that there should be a focus on users, consumption and user behaviour.

A new definition could combine aspects from the technological, cultural, systems-based and user-focused strategies. Ecological architecture could harness the power of new technologies and tools not solely to optimise and minimise, but also to advance social and cultural agendas. This could allow ecological design to become more architectural, towards specific strategies and processes that use a place-based approach.

Where there are local needs there are local experts, and flows of information, materials and energy are complex and ever-changing as technology directs innovation towards the biological.

HOK/Vanderweil, Process Zero: Retrofit Resolution (GSA building retrofit for *Metropolis* magazine's 'Get the Feds to Zero' competition), 2011
A network of systems operates in concert to maintain occupant comfort, provide ventilation, and generate power while minimising consumption. Solar thermal heats water for the radiant floor and domestic water heating. A geothermal system distributes cold water to chilled beams, which are fed conditioned ventilation air from a central energy-recovery unit. During swing seasons, these systems do not operate and the building is naturally ventilated.

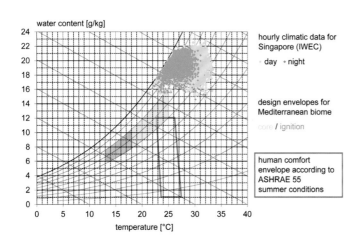

water content [g/kg]

hourly climatic data for
Singapore (IWEC)

· day · night

design envelopes for
Mediterranean biome

core / ignition

human comfort
envelope according to
ASHRAE 55
summer conditions

temperature [°C]

Transsolar Klimaengineering, Glasshouse Prototypes, Gardens by
the Bay, Singapore, 2011
For the National Parks Board in Singapore, Transsolar
Klimaengineering designed six 100-square-metre (1,076-square-
foot) glasshouse prototypes in order to study optimum growing
conditions for the plants, including temperature, humidity, air
movement and light, thermal comfort for visitors, and energy-
efficient design and operation of the glasshouses under tropical
climate conditions. Using dynamic thermal simulation with
TRNSYS, HVAC design with TRNSYS and EES, solar analysis and
on-site monitoring, the performance results from these studies
provided valuable data for the design of the large conservatories.

Applied Ecological Research

Designing with concern for the environment is a fundamental
part of architecture, yet architects are not currently positioning
themselves as leaders in the field of environmental design
or sustainability research. Despite the growing number of
research degrees in architectural subjects being established
and funded, it is proving difficult to develop and nourish a
research tradition in architecture that is integrated into both
the wider academic research communities of allied fields,
and into architectural practice. In contrast to academic
research, practice-based research is not always rigorously
defined or shared by peers. In academia, a goal of research
is dissemination, for example in peer-reviewed articles in
journals, specialist books and presented at conferences. In
architectural practice, dissemination of research is controlled,
and there is little motivation or method for architects to
disseminate their knowledge beyond their own offices and
clients.

There is an urgent need for new knowledge relating to the
global, multidisciplinary issue of sustainable design. Two main
ways in which architects are responding to the emerging brief
of sustainable building are firstly by bringing new knowledge
from outside the profession into design teams, and secondly
by attempting to create this knowledge from within the
design team or office. For example, it is now commonplace to
supplement the design team with consultants who specialise
in sustainable building, such as environmental engineers,
sustainability consultants and green building assessors.
Meredith Davey of Atelier Ten environmental engineers writes
about the firm's role in the Gardens by the Bay, Singapore
project with architects Wilkinson Eyre (pp 108–11). The
project involves the design of two artificial environments under
enormous glass domes that will allow visitors to have the
unusual experience of entering a 'designed' atmosphere, in one
area to experience a Mediterranean springtime with planting
including olive trees and grape vines. As Davey explains, the
research undertaken for the project was extensive and involved
multiple project partners.

Transsolar Klimaengineering was also extensively involved
in the Singapore project. Before building design even began,
Transsolar provided research for the client, the National
Parks Board of Singapore, in order to develop the building
brief by designing and constructing six 100-square-metre
(1,076-square-foot) prototype glasshouses. These cooled
buildings provided a research facility on site which allowed the
study of horticultural conditions, engineering, and architectural
strategies for thermal comfort for visitors and ideal growing
conditions for plants and trees in the proposed biomes.

This issue of △ highlights the emergence of design
practices that undertake sustainability research in-house. An
increasing number of architecture offices are developing new
sustainable building knowledge using internal consultancies
that they define as research groups, such as the Specialist
Modelling Group at Foster + Partners (pp 28–35), Aedas R&D
(pp 36–43), the Sustainability Group at HOK (pp 48–53, the
Nikken Sekkei Research Institute (pp 100–7), GXN at 3XN (pp
70–5) and the research team at Perkins+Will Canada
(pp 92–9).

The Emerging Brief

In the context of sustainable architecture, there is less focus on architects as creators of drawings, and more focus on architects as creators of different processes, activities and design outputs. The challenge of building sustainably has resulted in architects being asked to engage with new forms of communication, beyond the 2-D or even 3-D drawing. Clients are demanding that architects do certain works to include environmental considerations in new ways. With an increased focus on documenting energy, environment and various ideas of sustainability, architects are modelling, simulating and measuring buildings, energy and performance. For example, Foster + Partners have produced thermal energy studies in Masdar City, Abu Dhabi (pp 28–35), 2012Architecten regularly adapts ideas from industrial ecology to simulate energy and other flows into the site (pp 54–61) and 10 Design uses computational fluid dynamics to simulate the wind in its tower designs (pp 112–17). The cover of this △ is an abstract graphic generated from a digital simulation tool developed by Autodesk Research. The goal is to understand how air moves through a specific naturally ventilated space. This research aims to develop strategies to eliminate or reduce mechanical systems, which is a critical part of net-zero building design. A future workflow could see the architect as designing both the building and the flows of energy, light and air within it.

Measurements would seem to be an important part of assessing the sustainability of a design or building, but since there is no single agreed method or way of measuring or training architects to measure things like energy, airflows, carbon or material performance, the measurements are often a vague part of an architect's deliverables, with ranges of values and information from other consultants making up a significant proportion.

Architects BNIM are one of the offices featured in this issue of △ who use tools such as LEED and Living Buildings as a way of measuring their designs. Architect Laura Lesniewski explains the firm's approach to the Omega Center for Sustainable Living in New York (pp 76–81), one of the most progressive buildings in American architecture. It is the first building in the world to be certified LEED Platinum and have Living Building designation. While the building's ecological intentions are clear, its performance cannot be accurately measured until it is open, in use and tested in various ways over time. Simulating ecological and sustainable design and energy use at design stage, rather than using post-occupancy information or comparing before and after, remains the standard in the industry. There is no indication in the profession that this will change, despite the fact that clients, users and the public are unable to know if buildings really achieve the building performance that was simulated at design stage.

This approach poses a problem for ecological design: How can architects discover whether sustainable designs equal sustainable buildings? And of course it is impossible to conceive of a successful ecological building without ecologically mindful building users. People play a huge role in how buildings perform, and as Simos Yannas argues

Foster + Partners, Infrared Thermal Image Analysis, Abu Dhabi, 2010
top: Images taken with a thermal imaging camera in central Abu Dhabi showing the difference in radiant temperature in various spaces of the city. The tool was used to illustrate and assess how the design was able to lower the temperature.

Foster + Partners, Infrared Thermal Image Analysis, Masdar City, Abu Dhabi, 2010
above: Images taken with a thermal imaging camera showing the difference in radiant temperature generated by the design features of Masdar City. The tool was again used to illustrate and assess how the design was able to lower the temperature.

Number Of Floors: 45
Net to Gross: 0.83
Wall to Floor: 0.31
Floor to Ceiling: 3.88 m
Net Area: 89,700 m2
Gross Area: 108,300 m2
Occupants: 6400

Total Heating Consumption:	39	kWh/m2
Total Hot Water Consumption:	6	kWh/m2
Total Cooling Consumption:	50	kWh/m2
Total Fans/Pumps Consumption:	19	kWh/m2
Total Lighting Consumption:	36	kWh/m2
Total Small Power Consumption:	93	kWh/m2
Emissions Per Occupant:	1,500	CO2 kg/person/year

50.0 m
50.0 m

Ground Floor Footprint 2408 m2

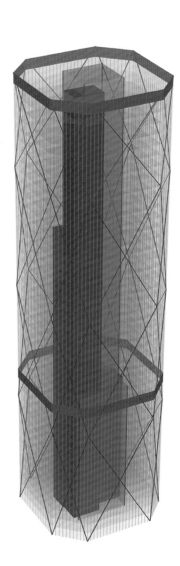

Concrete quality = C28/35

Core concrete volume = 11586.1 m3
Core concrete tonnage = 28965.4 tons
Core reinforcement volume = 193.2 m3
Core reinforcement tonnage = 1516.7 tons

Floors are not post-tensioned
Beam steel volume = 286.1 m3
Beam steel tonnage = 2245.9 tons
Floors steel volume = 138.2 m3
Floors steel tonnage = 1084.7 tons
Floors concrete volume = 12877.4 m3
Floors concrete tonnage = 32193.6 tons
Floors reinforcement volume = 53.7 m3
Floors reinforcement tonnage = 421.4 tons

Number of columns = 2670
Typical column section = HD400x900
Typical column section area = 0.1 m2
Columns steel volume = 1472.6 m3
Columns concrete volume = 0.0 m3
Columns steel tonnage = 11560.0 tons
Columns concrete tonnage = 0.0 tons
Columns reinforcement volume = 0.0 m3
Columns reinforcement tonnage = 0.0 tons

Foundation slab width = 62.5 m
Foundation slab depth = 62.5 m
Number of piles = 676
Foundation concrete volume = 12796.7 m3
Foundation concrete tonnage = 31996.8 tons

Total steel volume = 1896.9 m3
Total concrete volume = 37262.3 m3
Total steel weights = 14890.7 tons
Total concrete weight = 93155.7 tons

On Costs:	505 £/m2
MEP:	595 £/m2
Internals:	198 £/m2
Lifts:	185 £/m2
Facade:	275 £/m2
Superstructure:	653 £/m2
Substructure:	77 £/m2

Total Cost/m2:	2,400 £/m2
Total Life Cycle Cost:	6,600 £/m2/60 years
Total Maintenance Cost:	2,047 £/m2/60 years
Total Energy Cost:	4,630 £/m2/60 years
Total Emissions:	93 CO2 kg/m2/year
Total Embodied Energy:	750 CO2 kg/m2
Total Life Cycle Embodied Energy:	650 CO2 kg/m2/60 years

Aedas, Tall Building Simulation, 2009
This bespoke digital tool, programmed by Aedas and Arup running via Bentley Generative Components, provides an interactive platform to evaluate the consequences of shape, form and briefing decisions on the energy use, embodied energy and capital/life-cycle cost of a tall building early in the design process. Three initial drivers for any new development are defined first: footprint, occupancy and net area. Based on these, the tool then simulates the right number of floor plates taking into account required core size, structural dimensions and riser sizes. The generated form can then be manually adjusted to achieve local requirements and assess whether the achieved building mass is a viable reflection of the brief. The tool is the result of a collaborative partnership between Aedas, Arup, Hilson Moran and Davis Langdon.

(pp 62–9), creating adaptive architecture that responds to specific inhabitation and specific user needs is a necessary step towards a more ecological approach.

Ecological Design Beyond Buildings

Architects are a part of the ecology of a building project. This issue highlights examples of architectural initiatives that illustrate this emerging idea. Rau Architects proposes new supply chains and systems of ownership with the Turntoo initiative that allows clients to buy performance not products (pp 124–9). Thomas Rau predicts a future where buildings will be designed for disassembly and his office in Rotterdam has an experimental relationship with its suppliers, including a pay-per-lux contract with Philips. This is a case where the architect acts as the designer of the relationship between product and performance.

In an innovative energy-producing project, Rau creates an 'energy intranet' to connect the energy-generating roof on a college to serve a sports hall and housing on the site. Here, the office is designing an energy infrastructure as well as buildings.

Another example of architects designing processes and systems is from the Specialist Modelling Group at Foster + Partners. For Masdar City, the office presents a holistic energy strategy for an innovative scheme that straddles the scale of buildings and urbanism. Masdar is a design for individual buildings, but it works at an urban scale incorporating ideas of ecology, networks and systems-based design. Hugh Whitehead's and Irene Gallou's text (pp 28–35) contemplates the role of the architect as a generalist who must also be a specialist, and the role of research in the ecology of a design team.

Ultimately, *Experimental Green Strategies* illustrates emerging approaches to ecological design research that point to new ways of understanding ecological design. The future of applied architectural research lies in integrated, systems-based strategies of understanding ecologies at various scales, relating to design process, building and place. ∆

Notes
1. Ken Yeang, *The Green Skyscraper*, Prestel Verlag (Munich), 1999, p 31.
2. Ibid.
3. Aaron Betsky, *Out There – Architecture Beyond Building: 11th International Architecture Exhibition La Biennale di Venezia*, Marsilio (New York), 2008, pp 19–20.
4. Klaus Daniels, *The Technology of Ecological Building: Basic Principles and Measures, Examples and Ideas*, Birkhäuser (Basel), 1997.
5. Ibid, p 28.
6. Michael Lauring, 'From Ecological Houses to Sustainable Cities, Architectural Minds', in *The Nordic Journal of Architectural Research*, Vol 22, No 1/2, 2010, p 51.
7. Kevin Kelly, *Out of Control: The New Biology of Machines, Social Systems and the Economic World*, Addison-Wesley (New York), 1994, p 173.

2012Architecten, Harvest Map of New York, 2010
For each project, Dutch architecture office 2012Architecten uses its unique style of graphic representations of local material resources and energy flows called harvest maps. This harvest map of New York illustrates the flows of waste from New York City, considering the economic value (measured in dollars), the energy value (measured in megawatts), the landfill size (measured in feet high) and the quantity (measured in garbage trucks). One week's worth of city garbage requires a queue of garbage trucks equal in length to the New York City marathon track.

Municipal Solid Waste [%]

Statistics [per year]

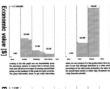
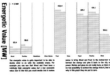
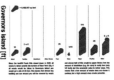
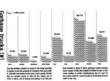

The NYC Waste Marathon

The amount of garbage trucks needed to dispose one week of garbage forms a queue occupying the full track of the New York Marathon.

DESIGNING AT

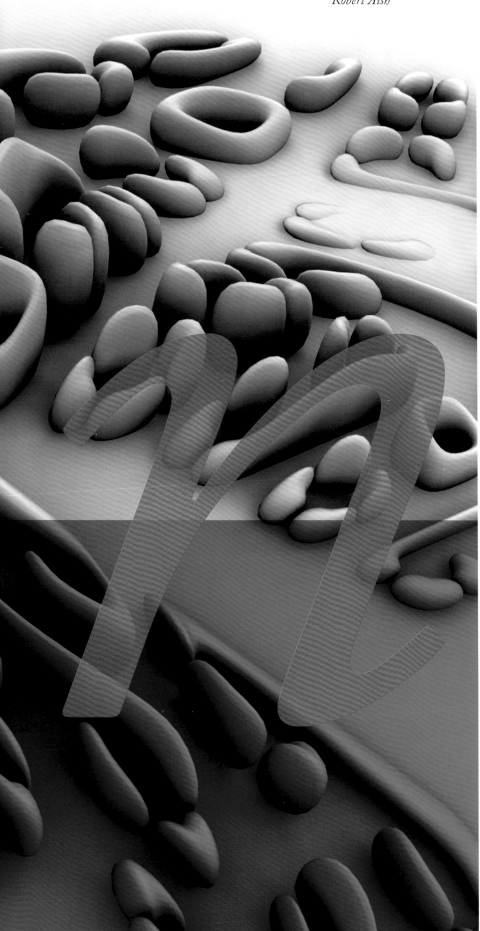

Method or Justification?
Zaha Hadid Architects, Kartal-Pendik
Masterplan, Istanbul, 2006. According
to the World Architecture Community:
'Parametricism is a methodologically
justified style that takes the concept
of using parametric design from the
production of one-off buildings and
applying it to a cityscape' (see http://
www.worldarchitecture.org/theory-issues/
index.asp?position=detail&no=253). One
of the important contributions of the late
Bruce Archer, former Professor of Design
Research at the Royal College of Art, was
his research into design methodology.
In his paper on the 'Nature of Research'
(1995), he distinguishes between
methods and value judgements. The
abstract concept of parametric design,
like other methods, is neutral. Buildings
and urban masterplans designed
parametrically may have attractive visual
properties and other positive advantages
in part facilitated by parametric design
tools, but a particular methodology or tool
set cannot be used as a way of justifying
the resulting style. In this context we
might conclude that the 'abstraction' (of
parametric design) at time t has become
a 'polemic' at time $t + n$.

Human Computer Interaction
Creator Ivan Sutherland using
Sketchpad around 1963 – the
origin of computational design.

In the last four decades, **Robert Aish** has played a pivotal role in the development of new technologies in architecture. As a professional software designer and developer, he has directly informed building design and processes. As Director of Software Development at Autodesk, his role is to converge innovative concepts such as design computation with mainstream design and engineering software. Also an influential disseminator of knowledge, he is a co-founder of the SmartGeometry Group and has helped create a vital bridge between architectural design and computation. Here he describes some of the critical dilemmas facing both software developers and architectural users of computational design tools, comparing the pioneering work of Bruce Archer and Ivan Sutherland in the mid-1960s (at time t) with how such tools are used today (at time $t + n$).

The concept of geometric transformation is at the root of computer graphics. However, many early CAD systems exposed the concept of transformation not as a single integrated idea, but via specific commands that controlled the constituent operations (scale, rotation and translation). Recent advances in parametric and associative design tools have directly exposed the abstract idea of geometric 'transformation'. If a progressive transformation is applied to a standardised profile or cross-section, then it is comparatively easy to generate the ubiquitous 'twisted tapered tower' that has become a familiar architectural form. Perhaps we could imagine a completely intuitive interactive analogue design tool for twisted tapered towers that encapsulates all the operations of a transformation. In this analogue modelling system the profile of the disperser nozzle defines the basic cross-section, and the hand–eye coordination of vertical translation and flow rate controls both the height, the scale and hence the taper. Rotation controls twist, and lateral translation controls shear. A coordinated 'wobble' combining rotation and vertical and horizontal translation introduces some interesting discontinuities. Through the use of this tool, the designer can harness transformation, but cannot acquire the concept of transformation. Do we want digital tools that mimic analogue tools, and mask abstractions, or do we want digital tools to be different to analogue tools and expose the underlying abstractions? The potential is there.

Software developers do not design buildings. Their role is to design the tools that other creative designers, architects and engineers use to design buildings. So while there is a level of indirection between the software developer and the resulting architecture, the perceptive software developer is deeply engaged in thinking about the process of design and about the architecture that results from this design process. He is also deeply concerned about the contribution that computational design tools can make and how designers interact with these tools: indeed, how the creative combination of tools and designers can make more appropriate, more responsive, architecture.

There seems to be a common thread linking architecture and computational design tools: both can be characterised by certain dualities. Do these dualities present inherent paradoxes or can these paradoxes be constructively resolved?

A building, for example, can be viewed as a system of interacting physical processes and also as a social and cultural artefact. In its symbolic role, a building can potentially communicate the fundamental basis of these interacting physical systems (for example, its 'eco-logic') or not.

There are parallels between architectural and computational design tools. If architectural design tools can be described as the discourse between the systematic and the symbolic, then computational design tools can be described as an equivalent discourse between the abstract and the intuitive.

Computational design tools can be viewed as interacting systems of programming abstractions and also as 'information artefacts' with their own 'culture of use' supporting human intuition. In its intuitive role, a computational design tool can potentially communicate the underlying computational abstractions or not.

These dualities also work over time. Concepts and technologies initially created and applied at one moment (at time t) are often subsequently used or interpreted in radically different ways (at time $t + n$). Indeed, there appears to be a drift (from t to $t + n$), from the systematic to the symbolic and from the abstract to the intuitive.

Flow rate = Scale

Vertical Translation = Height

....with coordinated wobble

Lateral translation = Shear

Rotation = Twist

The concept of geometric transformation is at the root of computer graphics

Shading or Styling?
Shading devices are an important tool of ecological design, but one can observe examples of shading devices that have been mounted on a north-facing elevation of a building in the northern hemisphere. What does this tell us about the designer's understanding of physics or of sustainability? What does the designer want to communicate to the lay public about the necessity to design buildings that efficiently respond to their environment? Have we not crossed the threshold from 'eco-logical design' to 'eco-illogical design'? Again, we might conclude that 'necessity' at time t has become 'decoration' at time $t + n$.

Do we design our buildings so that the public thinks architecture has apparently circumvented the laws of physics, or do we design our buildings so that the public understands how architecture has harnessed and responded to the laws of physics?

Ecological design is an important attempt to reverse this drift, by reasserting that a systematic basis for building design should be a primary consideration (not an afterthought). Ecological design also suggests that design tools (however intuitive) should present designers with appropriate abstractions of design, including those that relate to ecological design.

If we are searching for some 'datum' for design computation and design methodology, then perhaps the mid-1960s can provide a good example.

It is interesting that Bruce Archer's research into systematic design methods and design problem solving,[1] and Ivan Sutherland's pioneering parametric design software Sketchpad,[2] both appeared independently in the late 1960s. It was up to subsequent generations to appreciate the importance and complementary role of these two researchers. If computing is to be applied to a design process, then one needs a methodology of design. Conversely, it is difficult to apply a methodology (of design) without a suitable CAD system. These two researchers and the intersection of the ideas that they created has had a profound impact on the subsequent development of computation design tools and the application of such tools to architecture, industrial design and engineering.

In the 1960s I was a student at the Royal College of Art (RCA) and Bruce Archer was my dissertation supervisor. He introduced me to the nascent field of computer-aided design (CAD). As a result I was able to use one of the first commercial derivatives of Sketchpad, the PDP7 at Imperial College and at the Cambridge University Maths Lab under Neil Wiseman. The PDP7 used a similar vector refresh screen and light pen as Sketchpad. Although I was officially studying industrial design at the RCA, my interests included architecture, encouraged by my student contemporaries at the Architectural Association (AA).

The revolutionary aspect of Sketchpad was that it created an interactive constructive process that could be controlled intuitively by the direct manipulation of the designer. Many people who saw Sketchpad, or who viewed the archive videos, were initially attracted to the mechanics of interaction (the

The diagrid in the airframe of the Wellington bomber gave not only structural efficiency, but also sufficient redundancy

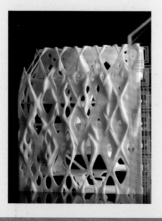

light pen, the interactive graphics) and ignored its essential underlying abstraction – its geometric constraint system. For many decades after Sketchpad, CAD implied 2-D drafting: that is, the representation of the results of design thinking. It is only comparatively recently that architecture has rediscovered the value of constraint systems as a way of representing geometric relations as a form of 'design intent', independent of particular geometric instantiations. There are other precedents for the rather tenuous and discontinuous relationship between technology and architecture. We might also ask how many centuries after the building of the Pantheon did it take before concrete was 'accidentally' rediscovered?

Let us consider the diagrid as a characteristic 'design pattern' of contemporary architecture. To manually model a diagrid is exhausting and the resulting design inconsistent. To write a script to generate a diagrid requires the designer to externalise his thoughts as an algorithm and forces him to design from first principles. However, once the script is written it is comparatively easy to play 'what ifs' and experiment with different grid options and different underlying forms: experimentation that would have been prohibitively exhausting with manual modelling. But if we take this process further, where it might be possible to simply press a button, access a menu and 'drag and drop' a diagrid on to the facade surface of our building model, then there is no need to think algorithmically, no imperative to design from first principles.

The example of the diagrid, the progress of its use and the progression of the related diagrid design tools raise some significant questions. Do we make design tools more intuitive so that the designer does not have to be confronted with underlying abstractions (algorithm or design principles), or do we make design tools more intuitive so that the underlying abstractions are more easily understood by the designer? In the latter case the use of the design tool has served an additional purpose. It has provided knowledge about geometric abstractions that goes beyond the specific building being designed.

Similarly with architecture: Do we design our buildings so that the public thinks architecture has apparently circumvented the

Generative or Evaluative?
DesignScript/Ecotect integration: a creative tool is one that unifies
different generative and evaluative aspects of design. One of the
key ways of facilitating ecological design is to integrate design
modelling, generative scripting and environmental analysis within
the same tool set. This enables designers to generate alternative
design solutions and evaluate these designs in a single process.

A truly creative tool is one that when used by a perceptive designer creates results beyond those envisaged by the original software developer.

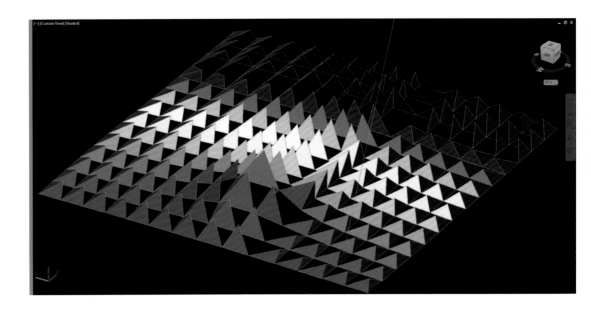

laws of physics, or do we design our buildings so that the public understands how architecture has harnessed and responded to the laws of physics? In both cases intuition plays an important role in making technology accessible to a wider public, but designers need to decide how we use this technology. Is it to create some (surface) impression or to give access to some (deeper) knowledge? How can a building provide knowledge (about ecological concerns and responses) that goes beyond the specific building being observed?

From the perspective of a software developer, we are designing an abstract artefact: a design tool. Tools transmit advantage from the tool maker to the tool user. Tools give possibilities, from these possibilities we discover advantages, advantages become a convenience, and convenience can too easily become a convention. Some tools, or the way some tools are used, make certain forms or processes 'convenient' and this can have a deeply conservative influence on design. There are alternative strategies. One is to make design tools that are more abstract and general.[3] These more abstract tools may not be so convenient to use: they may not provide predictable or convenient 'ready-made' solutions. They may require a deeper understanding on the part of the designer. But in so doing these tools free the designer from convention and thereby encourage exploration, and this brings us to another paradox. A truly creative tool is one that when used by a perceptive designer creates results beyond those envisaged by the original software developer.

Tools embody conceptual knowledge. Harnessing tools may relieve the designer of some physical and mental effort, but may also allow or suggest the acquisition of new conceptual knowledge. Therefore, never be limited by the available tools. Think beyond the tool. Tools should challenge the designer. The designer should challenge the tools. Become your own tool builder. Challenge yourself. △

Notes
1. Bruce Archer, 'The Nature of Research', *Co-design: the interdisciplinary journal of design*, January 1995, pp 6–13.
2. Ivan Edward Sutherland, 'Sketchpad: A Man-Machine Graphical Communication System', *AFIPS Conference Proceedings 23*, 1963, pp 323–8.
3. Robert Aish, 'DesignScript: Origins, Explanation, Illustration', in Christoph Gengnagel, Axel Kilian, Norbert Palz and Fabian Scheurer (eds), *Computation Modelling Symposium, Berlin 2011*, Springer, 2011.

Think beyond the tool.

Tools should challenge the designer.

The designer should challenge the tools.

Become your own tool builder.

Challenge yourself.

Foster + Partners, Beam Down pilot
project, Masdar City, 2008–
Aerial view of the 10-megawatt solar
panels at Masdar.

Hugh Whitehead, Irene Gallou, Harsh Thapar,
Giovanni Betti and Salmaan Craig

DRIVING AN ECOLOGICAL AGENDA WITH PROJECT-LED RESEARCH

Here **Hugh Whitehead, Irene Gallou, Harsh Thapar, Giovanni Betti and Salmaan Craig of the Specialist Modelling Group (SMG) at Foster + Partners** directly address the underlying premise behind the issue. They argue the case for the architect as generalist or 'centralised controller', coordinating an often specialised and diverse collaborative design team. As an in-house consultancy within Foster + Partners, SMS provides expertise in complex geometry, computer programming, parametric design and rapid prototyping and environmental simulation, aiming to provided directed specialist support whenever required.

To consider seriously the title of this issue is to consider seriously the assumptions that we hold while carrying out our work. Part of the role of an architect is to be a generalist, who coordinates the work of specialists in many different fields. To do this we continually engage in what might be termed project-driven research. But it is not research in the academic sense, where it must be specified, directed, reviewed and funded. It is more a continual process of enquiry and experimentation that is both open-ended and cumulative. There are no watertight compartments. We build a body of knowledge by promoting specific awareness, but always within a more general context.

By focusing on ecology we must first recognise that we are part of the ecology that we wish to study. With today's technology there is a broad spectrum of tools, techniques and approaches available to the designer. This includes parametrics, scripting and computation combined with analysis, simulation and relationship modelling. There is much debate about when to choose a top-down or a bottom-up approach. The reality is that we always start somewhere in the middle of what can be viewed as a series of nested systems, infinite in either direction. So we are not interested in moving up or down, but only in working out how best to move forward.

An Ecological Agenda in a Complex, Fragmented Industry

The design and production of physical artefacts and information systems today – from planes and buildings to software and business processes – is a complex, collaborative affair that involves thousands of participants working on different elements. The vastness and complexity of these projects mean that it soon becomes impossible for one single person to keep abreast of all developments. In these

Foster + Partners, View of the sky from open spaces, Masdar City, Abu Dhabi, 2008–
Stereographic projections of the obstructions as seen from a single point within a typical open space in Abu Dhabi and Masdar City. The sun path diagrams calculated from the latitude of the site are superimposed.

Foster + Partners, Specialist Modelling Group Focus and
Activities, 2011
Diagrammatical representation of the spread of the SMG skills
and research areas.

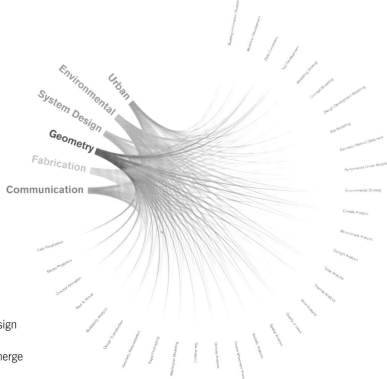

circumstances, it is natural for large-scale collaborative design
networks to take on a distributed form, where there is no
centralised controller. Global patterns of behaviour then emerge
as a result of concurrent local actions.

The construction industry is particularly fragmented.
For years commentators have expressed exasperation at the
adversarial nature of construction, citing the sheer number of
players involved in explaining the lack of accountability and
large number of disputes. They describe a building design
process which is wholly unsystematic, one that rolls on quickly
to meet programme deadlines, with design team participants
dealing with imperfect information and competing goals and
values.

The industry has become fragmented over many years,
with the growth of a number of specialists and consultants
– some of whom have interests only in very narrow areas of
performance – but now they fill an increasing gap between
designers and the end users of buildings. It is rare for a
common driver, other than profit, to emerge between the
different players. At least that is what a cynic would say.
An optimist could point to an ecological agenda gathering
momentum.

What is the role of research in implementing the ecological
agenda in construction? What questions should it answer, and
how? Who is best placed to carry it out, and when? Do we
need to focus our attention on generating new knowledge?
Or are our time and resources better spent transferring and
translating knowledge from other fields and industries?

These are important questions – questions that this
issue of $\triangle$ ought to lay groundwork towards answering. No
doubt more questions will be raised. The contribution here
is to describe how Foster + Partners Specialist Modelling
Group – through research and development – tries to act
on the ecological agenda of our time. The aim is to provide

a snapshot of a group with a diverse set of skills, trying to
balance a genuine commitment to environmental stewardship
with the – at times – unpredictable commercial commotion of
a rapidly evolving industrial ecology.

When is a Specialist a Generalist?
The Specialist Modelling Group (SMG) is an in-house
consultancy at Foster + Partners that was formed in 1997 as
a new department of Hugh Whitehead. Since its inception,
the idea has been to help design teams explore solutions
rapidly and then communicate data to clients, consultants
and contractors. To facilitate this process, the SMG has
continually fostered expertise in complex geometry, computer
programming, parametric design and – more recently – rapid
prototyping and environmental simulation. The SMG has made
a contribution to more than a hundred projects, including City
Hall (2000), the Albion Riverside residences (2003) and the
Swiss Re Headquarters (2004) in London, the Sage Gateshead
music centre in Tyne and Wear and Chesa Futura apartment
building in St Moritz, Switzerland (both 2004), and the new
Beijing International Airport (2008).

Foster + Partners, Typical Street, Masdar City, 2008–
Pedestrian circulation at ground level is through shaded colonnades
that can be screened to provide shade to low-angle sun and protection
from wind. At high level, mist jets humidify the air and make it cooler
on the ground.

*There is an element of pedagogy and
workflow consultancy in what the
group does. Sometimes there will be a
need to fill cognitive gaps and to help
designers interpret information and
the results of analysis from consultants.*

These seminal buildings were all a response to a directive
from Lord Foster to see projects as a vehicle for research and
an opportunity to explore new territory. So part of the brief
to the SMG has become to carry out project-driven research
and development within the intense design environment that
is the Foster + Partners office. One of the primary goals is to
develop control mechanisms that drive geometry in response
to relationships. These control mechanisms can be parametric
models or custom-programmed scripts. The CAD geometry
that the mechanisms are driving responds to the constraints
acting on the architectural design. Increasingly, the nature
of these constraints, performance parameters and design
criteria are becoming environmental. For example, we want
the benefits of natural daylight, but without the penalty from
excessive solar heat gain; which is the 'fittest' form?

A good way to resolve apparent conflicts is to develop
techniques that explore trade-offs – and this involves
interpretive skills. In-house consultancy and research by the
SMG aims to continually extend 'the art of the possible', but
also helps in the reordering of priorities. While much of the
energy goes into developing bespoke analysis tools, a project
is often best served by focusing on the issues of knowledge
transfer and translation to design. There is an element of
pedagogy and workflow consultancy in what the group does.
Sometimes there will be a need to fill cognitive gaps and
to help designers interpret information and the results of
analysis from consultants. At other times the most productive
contribution is in framing the issues so that there is an efficient
and coherent division of labour and flow of information
between the architect, SMG and external consultants.

In time, some of the tools used and developed by the SMG
may appear as a standard rather than a specialised part of the
architect's repertoire. Thus much of the group's time is spent
deciding what to focus on next. One challenge is how to better
'close the loop' between design and performance as built and
as used. How can we best capture the important information
and translate those lessons into the next project? This is crucial
if we are to tackle seriously the ecological challenge of our age.

Masdar: Intuition, Design, Analysis, Measurement
Masdar City is a unique 7-square-kilometre (2.7-square-
mile) economic zone and business cluster in Abu Dhabi, the
United Arab Emirates, powered by renewable energy, with the
aspiration for carbon neutrality and zero waste. The first six
buildings of the Masdar Institute campus – a clean-technology
research and innovation hub – are now complete.

The SMG was involved from the beginning of the design
process, paying particular attention to those aspects of
masterplanning, street design, materials and systems selection
that would have an impact on the way the campus was used

Foster + Partners, Thermal Analysis, Masdar City, 2008–
below: Comparative images showing the difference in radiant
temperature that these design features generate. A typical central
Abu Dhabi street photographed through a thermal imaging camera
shows bright white hotspots, and the street in Masdar Institute is
cool in comparison. The difference in radiant temperature of up to
20°C (36°F) is quite an achievement.

Foster + Partners, Felt Temperatures, Masdar City, 2008–
bottom: Shading, facade construction and materials can affect how
the temperature is felt by inhabitants. The creation of shade routes
encourages pedestrian activity at street level. The building's facades
have been developed to passively mitigate heat transfer while also
being highly sealed to minimise the energy required for conditioning
the internal spaces.

by its inhabitants, their thermal experience of the spaces, and
the energy consumption of the development.

Early research collected regional references to centre
the design culturally and historically. Contemporary urban
precedents (sparse, gridded asphalt highways walled by glass,
air-conditioned towers) were used as examples of what *not* to
do. A comparative review of socioeconomic studies of new and
old Arab cities – such as the Yemenite walled city of Shibam
– suggested that there was a strong correlation between
inhabitant density and per capita energy consumption: the
lower the density, the higher the consumption. Much of this is
to do with distance to travel, and the means of travel available.

With an unusually large number of consultants and
specialists on board, it became important to manage the
transfer of ideas and knowledge. The development of a strategy
for the urban microclimate is a case in point. The SMG's role
in these early stages was primarily in facilitating discussion,
framing questions for analysis, and assisting the architects to
respond appropriately to the results of analyses from various
parties. In this way a blueprint for a street orientation and
layout that shaded pedestrians and protected them from hot
winds was developed. This also led to a materials palette
and sectional form that distributed daylight intelligently, and
minimised the radiant temperature felt by pedestrians.

Sometimes great ideas and large swathes of intellectual
investment are wasted when attempts to communicate
their value to the client fail. The SMG put special effort
into translating all the consultants' technical findings into a
virtual-reality 'walk-through'. In this environment, the client
could see, for example, how the staggered streets blocked the
entry of the hot winds, which were modelled using data from
computational fluid dynamics (CFD) analysis.

The SMG has just completed its first post-occupancy
studies, using infrared thermography to understand how the
thermal experience of outdoor spaces at the Masdar Institute
compares with central Abu Dhabi. The debates between the
different groups involved in the design – from the core group
of architects to each of the satellite specialists – that this
survey has enabled have been particularly interesting. Viewing
the results of design decisions in that garish portion of the
electromagnetic spectrum is a great way to engage a wider
audience who, while having a large influence on the design,
may not have a grounded education in thermal physics.

Perhaps from this juncture there is an important distinction
to be made regarding ecological research. The question that
it raises is about the types of knowledge required to design
in response to the wider ecological challenge. Sometimes
pioneering knowledge generation is required. But most of
the time the reality is more mundane. Perhaps the biggest
challenge is about knowledge transfer: absorbing knowledge

Central Abu Dhabi

Masdar Institute

Felt Temperatures

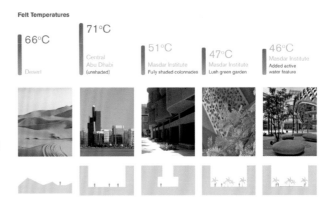

66°C — Desert
71°C — Central Abu Dhabi (unshaded)
51°C — Masdar Institute Fully shaded colonnades
47°C — Masdar Institute Lush green garden
46°C — Masdar Institute Added active water feature

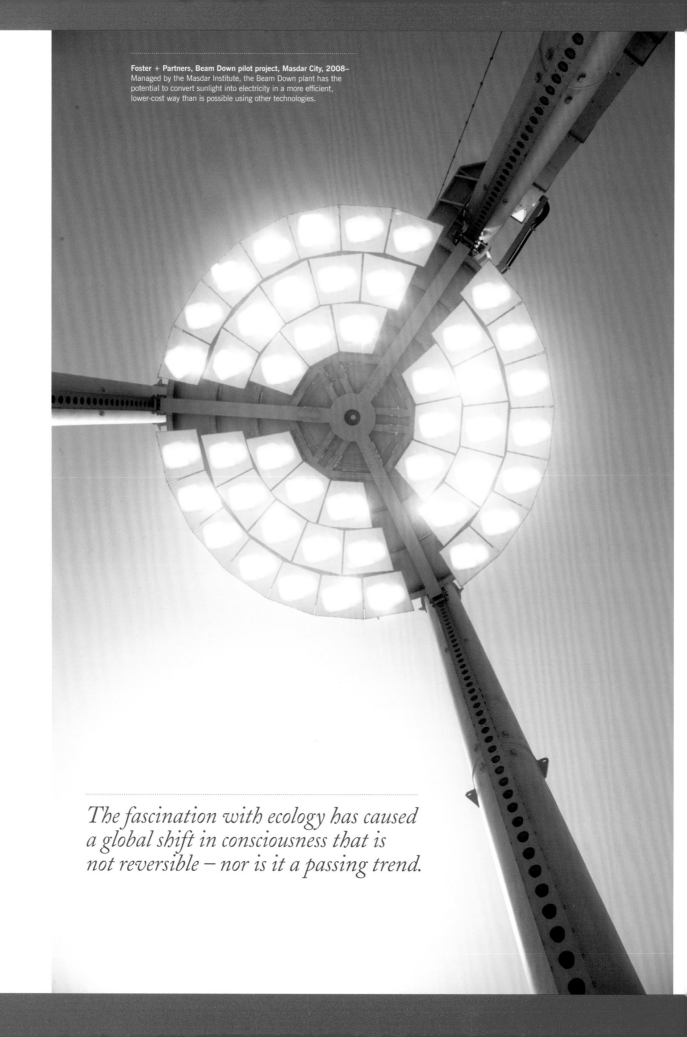

*The fascination with ecology has caused
a global shift in consciousness that is
not reversible – nor is it a passing trend.*

below: Diagram explaining how the Masdar Institute campus is powered.

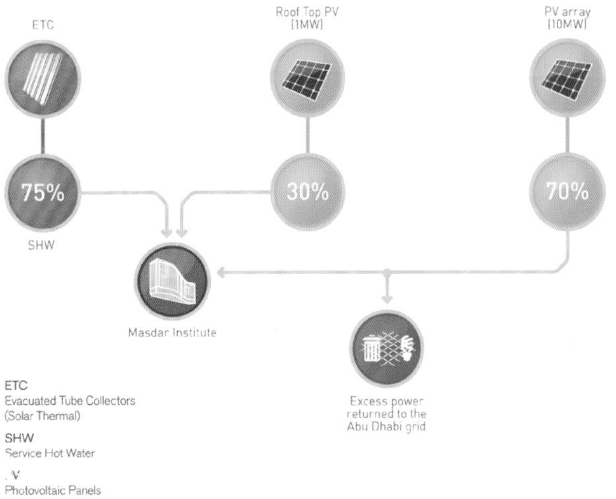

centre: Comparative images showing the difference in radiant temperature. On the hottest day of the year, people standing at various locations at the same time of day will perceive different temperatures.

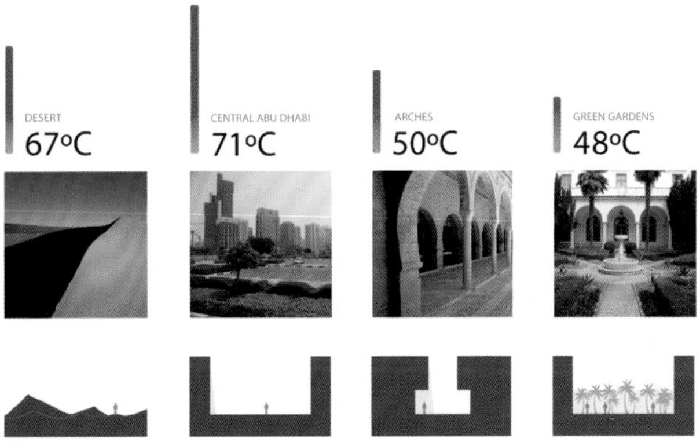

Foster + Partners, Wind Tower, Masdar City, 2010
bottom: A contemporary reinterpretation of a traditional Arabic wind tower brings cooling breezes into the courtyard.

fron... ; chewing
upor... translating it
into ... 'generalist'
desig... il is first
put to p...

The Future

Today's desi...
with which t...
It is exciting ...
if not thous...,
interrogatin... in a way th... is e...ndi... the ...
Playful experimentatio... ...ort... par... of inc...pora...ng
knowledge and exploring its limits. In ce......
it can even lead to the generation of genuinely new findings that can in turn be made in a form that is available for use by other designers. Yet it is also important to use the fruits of research and the impetus they provide to reflect and reorder our priorities. The wide-ranging debate on the place and nature of ecological research that this issue ought to spark is of course welcome. Let us not forget, however, that the ecological problems we face today are real; they demand a research agenda that is substantive, directed and clear-sighted.

The fascination with ecology has caused a global shift in consciousness that is not reversible – nor is it a passing trend. The posing of new questions has challenged and invalidated old and accepted solutions. The new thinking has also spawned new industries that in turn are having a beneficial effect on social and economic systems. What seems like a by-product is even transforming political agendas. This is not just a theory; the evidence is already becoming embedded and expressed in architecture. ∆

ETC

Roof Top PV (1MW)

PV array (10MW)

75%

30%

70%

SHW

Masdar Institute

Excess power returned to the Abu Dhabi grid

ETC
Evacuated Tube Collectors (Solar Thermal)

SHW
Service Hot Water

...V
Photovoltaic Panels

DESERT
67°C

CENTRAL ABU DHABI
71°C

ARCHES
50°C

GREEN GARDENS
48°C

Text © 2011 John Wiley & Sons Ltd. Images: pp 28–9, 34 © Oliver Jackson; pp 30–3, 35(t&c) © Foster + Partners; p 35(b) © Nigel Young/Foster + Partners

Christian Derix, Judit Kimpian,
Abdulmajid Karanouh and
Josh Mason

FEED
BACK

The specialist research and design unit in Aedas' London office focuses on three principal areas of research: computational design, advanced modelling and sustainable design. **Christian Derix, Judit Kimpian, Abdulmajid Karanouh and Josh Mason of Aedas R&D** explain how this cross-pollination of interests has led the practice to develop innovative approaches, exemplified by the design for Al Bahr Towers, the Abu Dhabi Investment Council Headquarters and the Digital Masterplanning (Digma) tool.

Aedas R&D, Al Bahr ICHQ Towers, Abu Dhabi, due for completion in 2012
The design integrates parameters of form, geometry and structure, shown
here for the curtain wall and dynamic shading screen.

ARCH
ITEC
TURE

As one of the world's leading practices, Aedas London invests in research and development (Aedas R&D) that has contributed to a shift in its output and character.[1] Aedas R&D's approach arose out of a desire to go beyond the automation of aspects of the design process to reveal spatial, environmental or construction qualities that lead to alternative approaches of design.

The evidence-focused agenda of the research group has established an approach to innovation where the tools and methods it creates are tested on projects against live constraints and deliverables. A key aspect of its work is the creation of collaborative platforms that bring together inspiration from disciplines such as engineering, finance, economics and psychology. The tools and methodologies it has developed provide feedback loops from design to operation that invite creative input from project teams. Through computation and computational tools, cross-disciplinary evaluation and design become seamlessly integrated, enabling Aedas to embed long-term environmental quality and performance at various design scales.

Aedas R&D focuses on three principal areas of research: computational design, advanced modelling and sustainable design. While a good proportion of the work relates specifically to Aedas projects, unique to the research group's approach is the ability to provide external consultancy and procure external research funding beyond the realm of architecture. Commissions from national and European funding bodies also allow the group to collaborate with universities and other industry partners, enabling it to bring academic research to live projects. Inherent in this is the commitment to share outcomes to promote the dissemination of

expert knowledge in the public domain and advance the industry as a whole. Examples of this methodology are the design of the Al Bahr ICHQ Towers in Abu Dhabi, currently under construction and due to be completed in 2012, and Aedas' investigations of the urban ecology of buildings.

Al-Bahr ICHQ Towers, Abu Dhabi

Having won the international design competition in 2007, Aedas London was appointed to design a landmark development for the Abu Dhabi Investment Council New Headquarters (Al-Bahr ICHQ Towers) in Abu Dhabi. For centuries, traditional Middle Eastern architecture has been well known for its sustainable features such as wind catchers, solar screens, cooling courtyards, ventilated domes and self-shading geometries. These features helped in providing comfortable spaces in regions subject to extreme weather conditions where temperatures can reach up to 50°C (122°F) and humidity up to 100 per cent. For the past two decades, however, curtain-wall glazing, more suitable to a temperate climate, has been the aspiration of the vast majority of projects in the Gulf Region,[2] resulting in the need for dark-tinted glazing and closed blinds, with occupants relying on artificial lighting throughout the day.

Inspired by Islamic and regional vernacular architecture, the design of the Abu Dhabi towers employs an adaptive kinetic shading screen as a dynamic Mashrabiya, a traditional wooden lattice shading screen particular to the Middle East. Controlled by the building management system, the dynamic Mashrabiya units will deploy into their unfolded state when a facade zone

Fully Closed   Half Open

Fully Open   Gradient Based On Sun Path

bottom: The intelligent building skin of Al Bahr
Towers is rooted in traditional Islamic architecture and
incorporates adaptive technologies via a biomimetic
design approach.

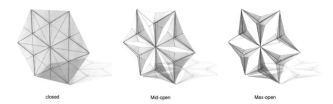

closed   Mid-open   Max-open

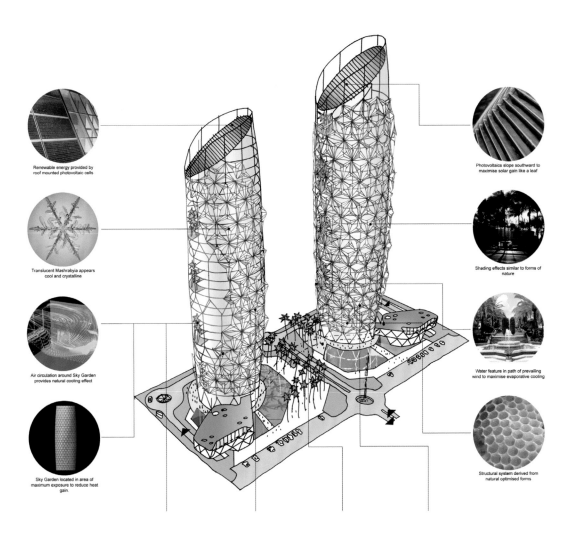

Renewable energy provided by
roof mounted photovoltaic cells

Translucent Mashrabiya appears
cool and crystalline

Air circulation around Sky Garden
provides natural cooling effect

Sky Garden located in area of
maximum exposure to reduce heat
gain.

Photovoltaics slope southward to
maximise solar gain like a leaf

Shading effects similar to forms of
nature

Water feature in path of prevailing
wind to maximise evaporative cooling

Structural system derived from
natural optimised forms

For centuries, traditional Middle Eastern architecture
has been well known for its sustainable features such
as wind catchers, solar screens, cooling courtyards,
ventilated domes and self-shading geometries.

Aedas R&D, Tall Building Model, 2008
Recent Aedas tall building projects that sparked the development of
the Tall Building Model, a parametric platform that gives interactive
feedback on the impact of design changes on cost, whole-life cost,
and operational and embodied carbon.

is subjected to direct sunlight. They will provide shading to the inner glazed skin and allow the building to adapt to its daily environment as well as the needs of its occupants. These dynamic tensile fabric structures will reduce glare and solar gain, lower cooling loads, allow views to the outdoors and bathe the floor plates in natural light. Through this intelligent system, and with the help of daylight sensors and dimmers, the use of artificial lighting can be significantly reduced. Overall energy consumption, carbon emissions and plant room sizes will be lower, and the glazing much more transparent so the floor plates will enjoy more daylight and vistas across the city.

A major challenge was managing energy performance and user comfort through the design process. With geometric rules underlying the design of the towers, the design team used algorithmic logic to enable communication through geometry and to negotiate the demands of each system. The floor-plate outline (defined by a series of tangent arcs) is scaled proportionally along an elevation curve and linked to drivers for improved building performance in terms of wind resistance, panellisation and solar performance. During design, any variations to these drivers would then propagate through the linked assemblies. This approach contributes to meeting the LEED Silver standard, with energy simulations carried out at key stages of design by Arup indicating a significant reduction in cooling loads. Drawing inspiration from vernacular architecture and designing more specifically to locality, the building expresses a whole-life approach to building performance and occupant comfort.

In parallel with this project, Aedas R&D continues to investigate the experiential drivers of contemporary low-carbon office design. Key to this is the burgeoning of a new type of 'global' office worker whose requirements are increasingly associated with the amenities of space, the environmental qualities of a 'networked' office and the urban infrastructure and identity[3] of the city. A recent study has brought together the lessons of a number of tall building projects to contrast the impact of a capital investment in integrated solutions to the long-term sustenance of the city through an urban identity of performance and form.[4]

Ecologies of Place

The Computational Design Research (CDR) group of Aedas R&D focuses on the interpretation and creation of design processes through algorithmic logic, regarding properties of spatial morphologies and its formation from a user-inhabitant perspective as the key to understanding sustainable environments. To this end, the CDR group has developed a bespoke spatial simulation framework as its primary crafting tool.

Ecology in urban design has a long history and was well defined by Magoroh Maruyama as a feedback or cybernetic system of apparently disparate sub-systems.[5] This operational paradigm was later extended to a sociospatial pattern generation logic by Bill Hillier and Adrian Leaman in the original Space Syntax approach,[6] later abandoned for analytical research of urban form. While recently developed commercial software like Autodesk's LandXPlorer support urban planning decisions, they generally

Aedas R&D, Digital Masterplanning: Spatial Planning, 2008–10
below: Spatial properties and design intentions can be encoded
as purpose rules into generative processes that inform the
configurations of places and simulate spatial planning procedures.
Many formation processes aim at land-use allocation and massing
design as seen in the four screenshots here.

Aedas R&D, Digital Masterplanning: Spatial Properties, 2007–10
bottom: Digital masterplanning analysis and visualisation
applications are digital tools that reveal spatial properties that
inform the value of the built environment. Many of these properties
are based on accessibility aspects such as movement structures,
network attributes or visibility.

tend to automate regulatory and quantitative performance criteria, which could be called 'constraint rules'. Urban design literature points towards 'morphological' design objectives of a discursive nature that are observable but rarely measurable.[7] These morphological objectives are called 'purpose rules'.[8] Purpose rules describe design intentions for the spatial configuration of a place – its morphological ecology – and mostly refer to properties of public space, perception of the space and the effect of its spatial structure on occupation.

Many of these observations resulted from the Smart Solutions for Spatial Planning (SSSP) project, funded by UrbanBuzz, a government knowledge transfer scheme for Building Sustainable Communities.[9] In collaboration with partners from academia, urban design and planning, Aedas R&D led the development of an urban design simulation framework. The framework – since extended and consolidated into Digital Masterplanning (Digma) – consists of a matrix of applications that allows designers to assemble bespoke design processes addressing design aspects and spatial performances at scales between area planning and architecture based on purpose rules. Particular emphasis for a sustainable place is given to access-related design aspects that inform spatial configurations. Hence many applications incorporate accessibility considerations that can be meaningfully encoded through algorithms and visualised in real-time: street-aspect ratios calculated on centrality measures and medial axes inform scales of buildings along roads; short walking distances between existing and planned centres of activity based on shortest paths generate active arteries and neighbourhoods; flow patterns for different modes of transport throughout a neighbourhood based on network calculations indicate land use and mix (and scales of noise and air pollution as well as boundaries); visual impact based on dynamic, volumetric intervisibility supports scale and orientation as well as passive surveillance and hence safety considerations; and vicinity maps based on skeleta and distance maps support decisions about space appropriation. Evolution and validation of the applications is consistent through feedback from implementation on projects such as the urban impact study for the Whitechapel Crossrail station in London, accessibility analysis for the MIST 340 neighbourhood of the Masdar Zero Carbon City in Abu Dhabi or the massing and access design for the Blackwall Reach Regeneration in Tower Hamlets, London. These simulations enable the understanding of civic attributes of places and inform values of locations within a masterplan that should ultimately reflect on a building mass adjacent to a public space.

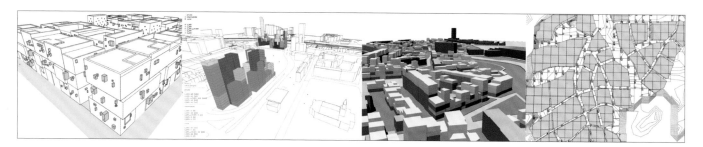

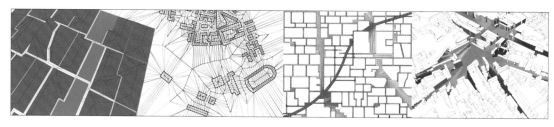

Aedas R&D. Crossrail Whitechapel Station Urban Impact Studay, London, 2009
below: Simulated views from locations moving along access routes approaching Whitechapel station in east London. The study was conducted for Crossrail in 2008 and helped identify the impact of locations of exits and street crossings on the urban environment. While the simulation can be observed dynamically exposing and integrating views, it compiles a gradient map as seen on the right in the digital masterplanning application diagram opposite.

Aedas R&D, Barclays Cycle Hire Network Usage Visualisation, London, 2011
bottom: Image from a visualisation of the routes taken by users of the Barclays Cycle Hire scheme in its first four months. Routes are calculated between the docking stations bikes are hired from and result in a time-based intensity mapping for flow, occupation of the city and reduced carbon emissions.

While all design applications have measurable performances, only some are evaluable according to regulatory constraints or development targets. Most qualities are related to observable performances visualised through the dynamics or states in the simulation, driven by the designer. It is therefore paramount for design simulations to allow identification with the purpose of computational process. This requires an operational and structural isomorphism between algorithm and design logic as well as accessible visualisation of the computational rules to reveal changes of states of design configurations. A split between evaluation and design generation therefore becomes problematic, since design intentions often cannot be intuitively associated with performance criteria. Designing sustainable ecologies of place needs to go hand in hand with designing transparent ecologies of computational design processes. A systemic approach must be represented via many lean, discrete processes associated to clear design aspects and their logic, negotiated by designers and guided by their intentions. In new computational workflows, instead of all-integrating parametric software, ecologies are produced by dialogues between many autonomous parts of which the designer is one element, just as they will be one citizen in a public space. ⌂

Notes
1. Aedas was named International Practice of the Year at the prestigious Architects' Journal Awards in 2010. Employing over 2,000 staff worldwide, it is the largest privately owned architectural practice in the world. This article was written with the aid of Abdulmajid Karanouh, Åsmund Gamlesaeter, Pablo Miranda, Steve Watts and Peter Oborn at Aedas. For more on Aedas R&D, see www.aedasresearch.com.
2. A Karanouh, P Miranda and J Lyle, 'Al-Bahr ICHQ Towers Solar Adaptive Façade', *Proceedings of the Adaptive Architecture Conference*, London, 2011.
3. A Schriefer, 'Workplace Strategy: What It Is and Why You Should Care', *Journal of Corporate Real Estate*, Vol 7, No 3, 2005, pp 222–33.
4. J Kimpian, J Mason, J Coenders, D Jestico and S Watts, 'Sustainably Tall – Investment, Energy, Life Cycle', in ACADIA 09: reForm(), 2009.
5. M Maruyama, 'Mutual Causality in General Systems', in JH Milsum (ed), *Positive Feedback: A General Systems Approach to Positive/Negative Feedback and Mutual Causality*, Pergamon Press (Oxford), 1968.
6. B Hillier, A Leaman, P Stansall and M Bedford, 'Space Syntax', *Environment and Planning B*, Vol 3, 1976, pp 147–85.
7. Commission for Architecture & the Built Environment (CABE), *By Design: Urban Design in the Planning System: Towards Better Practice*, Department for the Environment, Transport and the Regions (DETR) (London), 2000.
8. C Derix, Å Gamlesaeter, K Kropf, P Miranda and L Helme, 'Simulation Heuristics for Urban Design', in S Mueller Arisona, J Halatsch, G Aschwanden and P Wonka (eds), *Digital Urban Modelling and Simulation*, Springer CCIS (Heidelberg), 2011.
9. P Coates and C Derix, 'Smart Solutions for Spatial Planning – A Design Support System for Urban Generative Design', in M Muylle (ed), *Proceedings of the 26th eCAADe Conference*, University College of Antwerp (Antwerp), 2008.

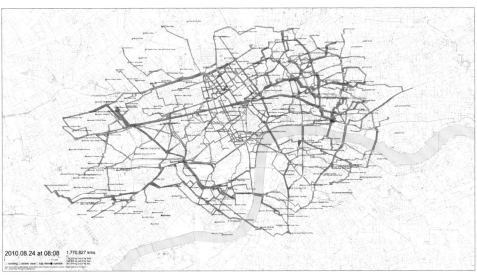

2010.08.24 at 08:08   1,770,827 kms

Co-founder of the Biomimicry Guild, Janine Benyus.

NATURE AS MEASURE
THE BIOMIMICRY GUILD

The potential for biomimicry lies far beyond the direct imitation of natural forms. Guest-editor **Terri Peters** describes how **Janine Benyus**, the biologist and innovation consultant, is using biomimicry to create performance metrics from natural technologies and processes for assessing aspects of ecological and sustainable design. The Genius of the Place study that she developed with the Biomimicry Guild, for instance, provides designers with a tool for exploring and reporting on the natural and environmental features of a specific site.

BIOMIMICRY DESIGN SPIRALS

© 2011 Biomimicry Group

1. **DISCOVER**
Natural Models

2. **ABSTRACT**
Design Principles

3. **BRAINSTORM**
Potential Applications

4. **EMULATE**
Nature's Strategies

5. **EVALUATE**
Against Life's Principles

1. **IDENTIFY**
Function

2. **DEFINE**
Context

2. **BIOLOGIZE**
Challenge

3. **DISCOVER**
Natural Models

4. **ABSTRACT**
Design Principles

5. **EMULATE**
Nature's Strategies

6. **EVALUATE**
Against Life's Principles

Biomimicry Guild, Biology to Design and
Challenge to Biology, 2011
opposite bottom: The Biomimicry Guild
has a biomimetic definition of sustainable
design, 'creating conditions conducive to
life for all human and natural systems'.

Biomimicry Guild, Life's Principles diagram, 2011
Life's Principles is a non-local, general code of conduct that
all designs should follow in order to achieve the guild's goal
that designs should not only respond to, and integrate into,
local ecosystems, but should also begin to create a surplus of
ecosystem services.

Evolve to Survive

Continually incorporate
and embody information
to ensure enduring
performance.

Be Resource (Material and Energy) Efficient

Skillfully and
conservatively take
advantage of resources
and opportunities.

Adapt to Changing Conditions

Appropriately respond
to dynamic contexts.

Integrate Development with Growth

Invest optimally in
strategies that promote
both development and
growth.

Be Locally Attuned and Responsive

Fit into and integrate
with the surrounding
environment.

Use Life-friendly Chemistry

Use chemistry that
supports life processes.

Evolve to Survive	Be Resource Efficient	Adapt to Changing Conditions	Integrate Development with Growth	Be Locally Attuned and Responsive	Use Life-friendly Chemistry
Replicate Strategies that Work Repeat successful approaches.	**Use Multi-functional Design** Meet multiple needs with one elegant solution.	**Maintain Integrity through Self-renewal** Persist by constantly adding energy and matter to heal and improve the system.	**Combine Modular and Nested Components** Fit multiple units within each other progressively from simple to complex.	**Use Readily Available Materials and Energy** Build with abundant, accessible materials while harnessing freely available energy.	**Build Selectively with a Small Subset of Elements** Assemble relatively few elements in elegant ways.
Integrate the Unexpected Incorporate mistakes in ways that can lead to new forms and functions.	**Use Low Energy Processes** Minimize energy consumption by reducing requisite temperatures, pressures, and/or time for reactions.	**Embody Resilience through Variation, Redundancy, and Decentralization** Maintain function following disturbance by incorporating a variety of duplicate forms, processes, or systems that are not located exclusively together.	**Build from the Bottom Up** Assemble components one unit at a time.	**Cultivate Cooperative Relationships** Find value through win-win interactions.	**Break Down Products into Benign Constituents** Use chemistry in which decomposition results in no harmful by-products.
Reshuffle Information Exchange and alter information to create new options.	**Recycle All Materials** Keep all materials in a closed loop.	**Incorporate Diversity** Include multiple forms, processes, or systems to meet a functional need.	**Self-organize** Create conditions to allow components to interact in concert to move towards an enriched system.	**Leverage Cyclic Processes** Take advantage of phenomena that repeat themselves.	**Do Chemistry in Water** Use water as solvent.
	Fit Form to Function Select for shape or pattern based on need.			**Use Feedback Loops** Engage in cyclic information flows to modify a reaction appropriately.	

Biomimicry in design is often unfairly associated with the stylistic imitation of natural forms, but Janine Benyus – the researcher who coined the term – believes a biomimetic approach is one that favours ecological performance research and metrics over shape making. Benyus co-founded the Biomimicry Guild with biologist Dr Danya Baumeister in 1998 and provides unique biological and innovation consultancy for design teams at Nike, NASA, Shell, the US Green Building Council, Arup Engineers, Gensler architects and others.

The guild recently formed a multiproject partnership with global design firm HOK to develop designs at the urban scale that integrate local ecosystems and have measurable environmental impacts and design goals. For example, in the design for a new development in Lavasa, India, with HOK, it helped develop building strategies that aid in rainwater management for the challenging site, which is subject to heavy flooding during monsoons. By observing the behaviour of the harvester ants on site, which design their nests in mud mounds that manage not to wash away, and studying and measuring the ways that the tree canopies on the site deflect rainwater, local knowledge was translated into usable ecological research. The biomimetic approach led the team to think about how to monitor and measure the site over a 20-year period, with the design aiming to reach different levels of maturity and impact over time.

Benyus is the author of several books on plant and animal adaption and natural technologies, including the influential *Biomimicry: Innovation Inspired by Nature* (1997).[1] It is in this book that she coined the term, and her work drew global attention from design professionals.

At the heart of its method is the guild's development of performance metrics from natural technologies and processes for assessing aspects of ecological and sustainable design. These ecological performance standards are different for each project, and are the result of site-specific ecosystem and biological research into the existing site, which allows the development of specific parameters and performance goals. Benyus explains that designers should rethink optimisation and efficiency as the main goals of a building design: 'Nature always doubles up on functions, think of a feather – waterproof, airfoil, self-cleaning, insulating, beauty for sexual reproduction. What can we expect from our buildings?'[2]

Benyus defines ecological design as place-based, taking into consideration a site's unique ecology and specific land type: 'Every building has to pull its ecological weight. Maybe we have a CO_2 storage metric to meet and we ask "Can the building sequester carbon in concrete based on the functions of coral?"'

The guild's work at the beginning of each project is in depth, local and involves multiple parameters, representing

Nature always doubles up on functions, think of a feather – waterproof, airfoil, self-cleaning, insulating, beauty for sexual reproduction. What can we expect from our buildings?

AskNature.org, Biomimicry Institute, Biomimicry Strategy –
Feather Structure Insulates: Canada Goose, 2011
left and bottom: Down feathers of geese insulate through special
architecture. Biomimicry taxonomy: maintain physical integrity,
protect from abiotic factors and control temperature. Biomimetic
application ideas: create more effective insulation instead of
manmade polymers, both in construction and clothing.

a new kind of design consultant with diverse ecological
expertise. It either consults with design teams, for example in
the planning of landscape, urban and architectural projects,
or joins them to integrate knowledge from within the team,
in a service it calls the Biologist at the Design Table. Benyus
also co-founded the Biomimicry Institute, a non-profit research
group that promotes biomimicry through resource sharing
and training. Her AskNature.org database is an initiative of
the institute, and is an online, open-source database about
biomimicry. Designers can browse and search by function,
for example biomimetic strategies for redistributing resources
or maintaining physical integrity, and it includes hundreds
of searchable data sheets with scientific references, photos,
details of experts and other relevant websites. Future plans
include the expansion of the database to include digital
drawing files and 3-D models that designers can share.

One of the important design tools that the Biomimicry
Guild introduces to design teams is its Genius of the Place
study, which begins with an exploration of the ecology of the
specific site; for example, perhaps it is on a flood plain or
experiences excessive heating or cooling, seasonal fires or
extreme weather. The guild then prepares a report that looks
at the various site-specific functions of the place, such as how
and where water is stored and purified, how waste is managed
on site, the economic development, local plant and animal

*One of the important design tools that the
Biomimicry Guild introduces to design teams is
its Genius of the Place study, which begins with
an exploration of the ecology of the specific site;
for example, perhaps it is on a flood plain or
experiences excessive heating or cooling, seasonal
fires or extreme weather.*

life, and other factors. Benyus looks to the rocks, plants, soil,
animals and other life for inspiration: 'How are the local plants,
animals, ecologies coping in this environment?' The report
goes beyond typical checklist-style site investigations because
it is tailored to the specific ecological culture of a place and
observes, measures and discovers how life behaves on the
site over time. It helps focus the design team on larger issues
that can have a huge environmental impact at the beginning
of a project, which leads to a study of 'best practice' – looking
to nature for inspiration in a focused, detailed and scientific
approach. ⌂

Notes
1. Janine M Benyus, *Biomimicry: Innovation Inspired by Nature*,
William Morrow Publishers (New York), 1997.
2. Conversations between the author and Janine Benyus on 22
February and 11 June 2011.

Mary Ann Lazarus and Chip Crawford

RETURN GENIUS TO THE

Mary Ann Lazarus and Chip Crawford

ING
PLACE

HOK and Buro Happold, Khed Special Economic
Zone (SEZ), Maharashtra, India, 2009–

Advocates of sustainable design since the early 1990s, HOK are intent on disseminating new research, resources and tools across their global design teams. **Mary Ann Lazarus**, Sustainable Design Director at HOK, and **Chip Crawford**, Planning Group Director at HOK, describe a particularly innovative project that the two groups have collaborated on with the essential input of the Biomimicry Guild (see p 44). Addressing critical environmental issues at the habitat scale and performance standards, they have developed ecological design tools that have been employed on masterplans for Lavasa, India, and Langfang, China.

Global architectural design office HOK was an early adopter of both sustainable design and ecological design research. The firm's initiative in green design has proved formative for North American architecture. Key members of the practice were instrumental in establishing the US Green Building Council in the early 1990s, which helped propel sustainability from the fringes into a significant mainstream movement. Now in its second edition, *The HOK Guidebook to Sustainable Design* is an influential manual used by both design professionals and students.[1]

HOK is increasingly using ecological feedback to emulate not just nature's appearance, but also to shape performance. The principles of biomimicry and place-based ecological design analysis are used, for example, in large-scale urban projects by the HOK Planning Group. The firm's approach to communicating sustainability research is to decentralise the knowledge and let it percolate across its design studios and among its large global staff. The work of the Sustainability Group provides new research, resources, processes and design tools that are shared on a collaborative sustainable intranet site.

In 2008, HOK began collaborating with the Biomimicry Group (see pp 44–7), an independent, bio-inspired research consultancy led by biologists and based in Helena, Montana.[2] Together they aim to integrate highly evolved forms and systems found in nature into the planning and design of buildings, sites and cities.[3] The HOK Planning Group currently covers a land area of about 12,950 square kilometres (5,000 square miles) in its masterplanning strategies (approximately the size of the state of Connecticut). Biomimicry addresses critical environmental issues at the habitat scale, and the hope was therefore that combining design with biology could create significant results – even restorative outcomes – at all scales. The planning group has served as the Petri dish for assimilating biological thinking into the firm's work, which is steadily being embraced by its architects.

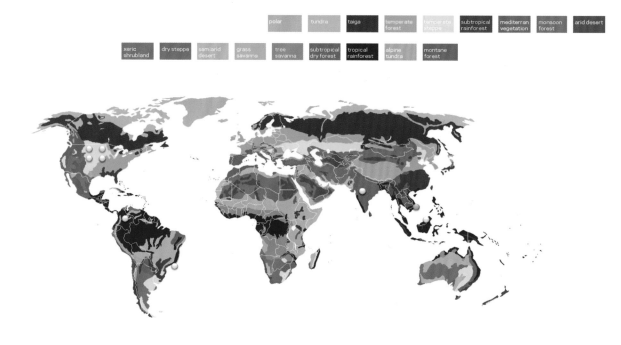

HOK and Buro Happold, Khed Special Economic Zone (SEZ), Maharashtra, India, 2009–
The FIT problem-solving methodology helped the team planning the Khed SEZ ensure that the plan drew from nature's proven design solutions to create buildings and communities that function like natural systems in the local biome. A biome describes a type of climate and vegetation that exists in specific regions throughout the world. The Biomimicry Group has selected a biome classification system that is a derivative of the World Wildlife Fund classification of terrestrial ecosystems and that describes 18 biomes. The climate for the Khed SEZ in Pune, which is near India's west coast, has commonalities with areas of South America and Africa, but with clear geographic distinctions. In this biome, deciduous forests predominate.

Key ecological design tools that have been developed with the Biomimicry Group and used on projects such as masterplans in Lavasa, India, and Langfang, China, include ecological performance standards, 'genius of the place' analyses of a site's unique natural systems attributes and what local organisms are doing to leverage their environment, and the Fully Integrated Thinking (FIT)™ living systems design tool.[4]

Modelling Ecological Landscapes: Lavasa, Western India

For the new hill town of Lavasa, just outside the major city of Pune, the HOK-Biomimicry Group team created an ecological landscape model to generate site data from which to develop design tools, strategies and methods to address sustainability. The research revealed that the local biome was a moist deciduous forest, a natural habitat that has been erased by more than 400 years of slash-and-burn agriculture. This complex site receives up to 9 metres (29.5 feet) of rain in three months and is then dry for most of the year.

The team identified the six most important ecosystem services to measure in the biome: water collection and storage, solar gain and reflection, carbon sequestration, water filtration, evapo-transpiration, and nitrogen and phosphorous cycling. If the new Lavasa development changed just one of these layers making up the newly revitalised forest, the ecosystem would be disturbed. To prevent this from happening, the design team established strict ecological performance standards and specific strategies for maintaining each ecosystem service. The key concept informing the landscape masterplan for the Lavasa valleys was thus the sustainable role of the native forest ecosystems in the region's water and soil cycles.

The genius of the place report for the area allowed the team to set ecological performance standards and then to create biome-specific strategies. The findings regarding the moist deciduous forest show that during the region's monsoon season, 20 to 30 per cent of the water evaporates back up into the clouds due to the tree canopies. This evaporation is critical because it helps drive the precipitation inland. It is therefore important that the built environment of the new community replicates the functional effect of the moist deciduous forest. Design strategies include roof lines that create the wind turbulence that aids the evaporation, green roofs that prevent soil erosion, and using a polymer product that stiffens soil to create the same stabilising effect as cliff swallows mixing saliva with mud to create mortar that adheres their nests to buildings. Based on the forest model, the landscape design must allow for the 10 to 15 per cent surface runoff through integrated stormwater management and the 60 to 65 per cent infiltration through building and site design.

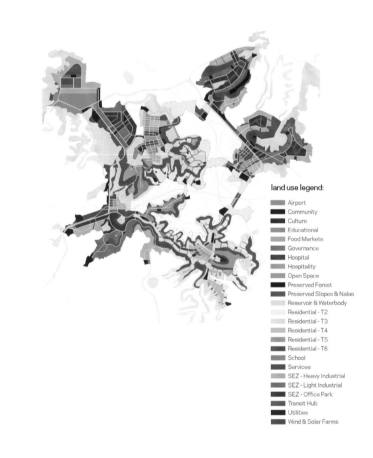

land use legend:

- Airport
- Community
- Culture
- Educational
- Food Markets
- Governance
- Hospital
- Hospitality
- Open Space
- Preserved Forest
- Preserved Slopes & Nalas
- Reservoir & Waterbody
- Residential - T2
- Residential - T3
- Residential - T4
- Residential - T5
- Residential - T6
- School
- Services
- SEZ - Heavy Industrial
- SEZ - Light Industrial
- SEZ - Office Park
- Transit Hub
- Utilities
- Wind & Solar Farms

top: Working with Janine Benyus and the Biomimicry Group, the Fully Integrated Thinking (FIT) design tool helped the HOK team develop a comprehensive framework that, with biomimetic design principles at the heart of the plan, addresses the natural and manmade systems to achieve environmental, social and economic sustainability. The team established specific goals and performance indicators for each of the 15 FIT 'lenses', such as water, materials, energy, education and governance, which are used to measure performance during design, construction and operation.

above: Land-use masterplan. The composite land-use plan of Khed SEZ illustrates a land-use pattern that is highly organised, strategic, and balances high concentrations of activity with less intensive land use and areas of conservation. Many of the uses are interdependent upon adjacent activities, creating neighbourhoods that are functional and vibrant.

Eco-Smart City Masterplan: Langfang, China

Working with the Biomimicry Group, as well as the Woods Bagot architecture firm and other consultants, HOK developed an eco-smart city masterplan for Langfang, located in the dynamic Beijing-Tianjin metroplex in the North China Plain. Using nature as its guide, the plan is intended to renew the existing city to create a healthy eco-structure, a healthy economy and healthy people, setting a new example for all Chinese cities.

Formed through alluvial actions, the plain on which Langfang sits lost its native mixed deciduous broadleaf forest 4,000 years ago and instead has functioned as an agricultural plain. This has drained the natural aquifer once found beneath the alluvial soils. Today, one of Langfang's biggest challenges is that drought and single-family farming have caused a tremendous decline in water quantity and quality, and the water table is falling 1.5 metres (4.9 feet) a year. Meanwhile, the three rivers coming from the Beijing watershed are bringing pollution to the area.

The Fully Integrated Thinking (FIT) design methodology, or living systems design tool, was developed by HOK and the Biomimicry Group to help address the entire spectrum of environmental, social and economic systems. FIT enables design teams to address projects through 15 categories, or 'lenses', which work together to achieve triple bottom-line results. These manmade and natural lenses are eco-structure, water, atmosphere, materials, energy, food, community, culture, health, education, governance, transport, shelter, commerce and value. It thus serves as a flexible framework that helps in the organisation and analysis of data about the categories designers want to address.

The Langfang plan brings the lives of its people and nature together through the formation of a green belt, through compact development, water restoration, the establishment of eco-corridors and by creating a cultural identity. Rather than accepting a south-to-north pipeline that could bring in water from the Yangtze River, the design team recommended that Langfang instead work towards establishing a self-reliant, functionally balanced water cycle that recharges the aquifer. The hope is that by introducing blueways and greenways in channels that restore the natural functionality of areas where water previously flowed for millennia, the plan will trigger cultural and economic restoration to enable the area's people to better support themselves. In addition to providing water for farming, the blueways contribute to recreational uses and economic development through tourism.

Advancing FIT and Connecting with Other Research Partners

No single design firm has the capacity to fully address each of the 15 FIT lenses. Many, like water, food and energy, are entire industries. For this reason, the HOK-Biomimicry Group team is actively seeking research partners, especially universities, to engage with its FIT research.

John Shreve, a HOK Planning Group urban designer, is currently applying FIT to study the intersection between culture and design while participating in a PhD programme at the University of Kansas (KU). With the baby boom population reaching retirement age, Shreve is leading a FIT-focused effort to study how community development and lifestyles will change in coming years. HOK and KU are seeking to develop a mutually beneficial relationship in which the university is able to partner with outside experts and HOK can use KU as a special R&D lab for FIT.

Growing Together

It is not in the natural rhythm of architects to consult with biologists before they begin designing. HOK's designers, however, have discovered that whether it is building structural systems that retain water like tree roots, or creating a building structure mimicking the canopy layer in a forest, this can lead to inspiring ideas they never would have considered before.

HOK has identified a need to redesign information flows and project teams as a result of ecological research. This focus on bio-inspired performance requires new methods of organising project teams and a less linear design process. In this new line of thinking, biologists join planners, architects and other professionals early in the design process.

Truly bio-inspired building design – as opposed to the biomorphic design of the Bird's Nest Olympic Stadium in Beijing – is still in its infancy. However, HOK expects adoption to grow exponentially when clients start to see the performance of built projects that have integrated biomimicry. The team is particularly enthusiastic about a future building project in South America that it says will be beautiful, high performing and 'generous' in the way it gives back to the community.

Notes

1. Sandra Mendler, William Odell and Mary Ann Lazarus, *The HOK Guidebook to Sustainable Design*, John Wiley & Sons (Hoboken, NJ), 2nd edn, 2006.
2. 'Biomimicry Guild, HOK in Alliance', *Environmental Building News*, 1 December 2008; see www.buildinggreen.com/auth/article.cfm/2008/11/24/Biomimicry-Guild-HOK-in-Alliance/.
3. A discussion between Dr Dayna Baumeister, Chip Crawford and Mary Ann Lazarus about this partnership can be found at www.youtube.com/watch?v=wr6XFQJjO-U.
4. HOK and the Biomimicry Group developed the FIT problem-solving methodology. Rooted in life's principles, this Fully Integrated Thinking tool draws from nature's proven design solutions. FIT places life at the centre of a team's decision-making so that designers can create buildings and communities that function like natural systems. It helps design teams address the entire spectrum of environmental, social and economic systems.

Moist deciduous forest function.

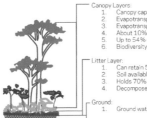

Canopy Layers:
1. Canopy captures and evaporates 10 - 30 % of rainfall
2. Evapotranspiration rate of 60 mm per month in wet season
3. Evapotranspiration rate of 40 mm per month in dry season
4. About 10% of incoming light reaches the ground in the wet season
5. Up to 54% of incoming light reaches the ground in the dry season
6. Biodiversity of 30 to 100 different native tree species per hectare

Litter Layer:
1. Can retain 51% of rainfall during the monsoon (75% during dry season)
2. Soil available water capacity 35 - 65%
3. Holds 70% of all nutrients deposited in the forest
4. Decomposes in 7-8 months

Ground:
1. Ground water recharge is 10% of total rainfall

Existing forest rainwater model.

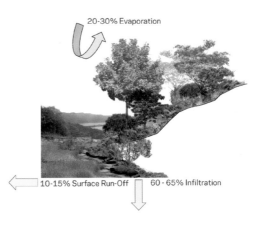

20-30% Evaporation

10-15% Surface Run-Off   60 - 65% Infiltration

Built environment rainwater model.

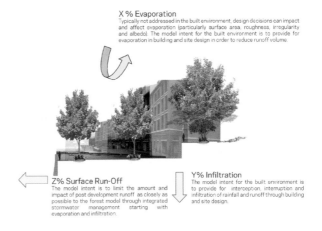

X % Evaporation
Typically not addressed in the built environment, design decisions can impact and affect evaporation (particularly surface area, roughness, irregularity and albedo). The model intent for the built environment is to provide for evaporation in building and site design in order to reduce runoff volume.

Z% Surface Run-Off
The model intent is to limit the amount and impact of post development runoff as closely as possible to the forest model through integrated stormwater management starting with evaporation and infiltration.

Y% Infiltration
The model intent for the built environment is to provide for interception, interruption and infiltration of rainfall and runoff through building and site design.

HOK, Lavasa Hill Station, Lavasa, India, due for completion in 2012
opposite bottom and above: Genius of the place report on how organisms on this challenging site – a community in the 971-hectare (2,400-acre) Mugaon mountain village outside Pune, which experiences a three-month monsoon season followed by nine months of almost desert-like drought – have survived over time.

2012Architecten, Villa Welpeloo, Enschede, The Netherlands, 2009
The materials identified using the harvest map resulted in new shapes and methods of construction. The inner parts of cable reels were used for the facade, and the load-bearing construction is made from steel beams from a paternoster textile machine.

RECYCLICITY
A TOOLBOX FOR RESOURCE-BASED DESIGN

*Jan Jongert, Nels Nelson
and Fabienne Goosens*

Architect Jan Jongert, urban ecologist Nels Nelson and chemical engineer Fabienne Goosens of 2012Architecten are all part of a shifting cast of specialists, undertaking research and design in this Rotterdam-based practice. Here they describe how a focus on recycling has led them to develop research tools, such as harvest maps, urban metabolism studies, material flow analyses and Sankey diagrams. These provide essential information for designers. Harvest maps, for instance, enable them to locate locally available recyclable materials and resources.

Cities have grown into conglomerates of mono-functional districts that hardly relate to each other. Business districts, industrial zones, agriculture, housing and commerce are spatially restricted and rarely benefit from the presence of one another. The increasing amount of in- and outgoing flows of goods, energy, water, food and even capital are unrelated and contribute to limitless transport, local clogging of traffic, loss of energy, and increase in waste and pollution. There is thus a need to research alternative strategies for integrated urban planning.

2012Architecten's activities are directed towards the creation of symbiotic architectural environments. Its Recyclicity[1] concept operates from the conviction that transforming the existing unconnected city into a healthy ecosystem will turn it into a resilient environment with different actors profiting from each other. Taking inspiration and knowledge from industrial ecology, 2012Architecten's built architectural examples, such as Villa Welpeloo in Enschede, The Netherlands (2009), demonstrate the potential of resource-based design. The firm uses research tools such as harvest maps, studies of the urban metabolism of the city, material flow analysis and Sankey diagrams to continuously develop, communicate and analyse ecological design possibilities that include recycling at all scales.

2012Architecten, Superuse.org, 2007
Superuse.org is a platform for designers to exchange ideas on adaptive reuse for art, design and architecture.

2012Architecten, WORM Rotterdam Harvest Map, 2010
The harvest map illustrates the regional sourcing of building materials for the WORM cultural platform in and around Rotterdam. WORM was constructed in 2005 and opened 2006.

2012Architecten, Villa Welpeloo, Enschede, The Netherlands, 2009
A harvest map can reveal locally available material sources, derelict buildings and wastelands, potential energy sources (heat/cold and electricity), unused food production facilities and derelict infrastructure. The map indicates geographical position, amounts, dimensions, availability and potential for each source.

Harvest Maps

Since 1997, the office has focused on investigating the architectural applications of urban and industrial waste material flows. Superuse is a design strategy that uses local materials considered as waste or as being of no value and gives them a new function in buildings, interiors and products. The strategy involves using as little energy as possible for transport and transformation into the new design.[2] One of the most helpful tools is the harvest map, a drawing indicating the available supply of materials in the vicinity of a building project. For an architect, the harvest map functions as a regional material catalogue that can be used to assist the design team and also to communicate material choices to the client. Harvest maps have since formed the basis of most of 2012Architecten's designs, such as the extensively published Villa Welpeloo, a new single-family home clad with reused timber from local cable-reel storage, and reused steel from abandoned machines from the local textile industry.

Urban Metabolism Flows:
Physical, Information and Strategic Layers of the City

Many potential resources are constantly moving into and out of a city system. In order to gain an understanding of this 'urban metabolism', 2012Architecten has conceptually mapped available resources in layers. A primary layer consists of physical movements of energy and materials, such as heat, traffic, water, materials, products, buildings and food. The information layers contain flows of knowledge, money, material and company culture. This includes different types of data that are flowing through different channels in the urban system and are used in short-term economic decisions, driving exchange of feedstock, products, utilities and services. Next to knowledge and company culture, money is included here because its role in society is often one of information; for example, the price of a product gives information about its value in society. The strategic layers relate to flows of people, nature and labour. This includes all private and public stakeholders that decide on and influence the structure of the network and drive its evolution over time by providing feedback loops.

Strategies for improved networks in urban supply chains can either be resource-based or target-based; that is, based on what is already offered in the system or what is ideally demanded from it (a utopian blueprint). Because the firm does not believe in tabula rasa development or that total autarkies contribute to sustainable communities, its Recyclicity concept favours instead the resource-based strategy.

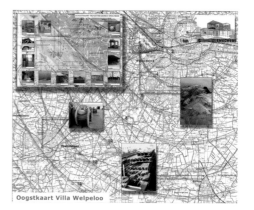

Oogstkaart Villa Welpeloo

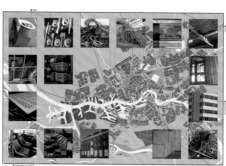

Cyclifiers

Cyclifiers, a typology codified by 2012Architecten,[3] are short-circuited resource-recovery and reuse mechanisms with spatial and public features. They plug into locally available but unused resources, addressing the various layers of urban flows by acting as metabolic processors. They comprehend, sort out, select, integrate, coordinate and cohere.[4] This helps reverse the urban tendency to disperse materials and energy until the value is lost to the surroundings, unable to be retrieved or recycled back into the system.

A cyclifier is not conceived of as a hybrid system – which has become a trend in contemporary architecture (an example of which is OMA's De Rotterdam mixed-use vertical city, 1997) – because a hybrid attempts to create an entire universe in one building. Rather than independency, cyclifiers try to reach the maximum possible interaction between existing activities with as few as possible adaptations to the existing fabric. The concept is in this sense closely related to 2012Architecten's Superuse. Both have the goal of redirecting, transforming and connecting local existing materials and energy flows, and adapting the system to local circumstances, and cyclifiers also take into consideration the information and strategic layers of the city.

Modelling Urban Symbiosis

The complexity of the urban metabolism demands a clever way of representing and communicating these interactions in order for the data to be used as a design tool. 2012Architecten utilises two well-developed representation methods to analyse and understand the structure of the city. Material flow analysis (MFA) is a structured methodology for comparing infrastructure scenarios and was developed in the field of industrial ecology. MFAs are able to analyse systems on different layers at the same time.

The office also uses a more graphical representation of urban flows called Sankey diagrams, which were invented in the late 19th century to visualise energy efficiency in industrial processes. The diagrams use arrows to show flows, and are graphically distinctive because the width of the arrow is proportional to the flow quantity. They can be used to show both the relationships and directions of energy flows as well as the relative volumes passing through the urban context, enabling the design team to visualise and understand the performance of all metabolism flows and to interfere with them in a design.

Organic food market, Seoul, 2010
below: An organic food market in Seoul is
located in a subway car to bring the flows
of food and commuters closer to each other.

2012Architecten, Renovation Strategy for the Faculty of
Architecture, Delft University of Technology (TUDelft), The
Netherlands, 2010
bottom: Sankey diagram showing the current flows of water entering
and leaving the building. The second image shows the suggested
diverted flow of rainwater to be used as flushing water for toilets.

Case Study: Sustainable Development of a Shrinking City

In 2009, 2012Architecten began testing and researching the cyclifier concept using a case study for proposing future transformations in three shrinking neighbourhoods in the region of Heerlen in the Netherlands. The MSP2040 study focused on the analysis of the metabolism of the site, the potential for energy and other flows to be short-circuited/looped, and on the spatial implications of their reintegration. The area was dependent on local industry, and since the local mines were closed in the 1970s the neighbourhoods have experienced various socioeconomic problems. The region's population has been declining and is expected to continue to do so in the future.

The design challenge was how to use design tools to map resources and urban flows and respond to the challenge of a shrinking city. Government funding is available to allow the transformation of such areas and 2012Architecten was one of five architectural offices commissioned to design future visions of Heerlen as a sustainable city in 2040. A series of data sources, strategies and tools were developed to help positively integrate future transformation of the site. Drawing on the office's interest in, and knowledge of, the application of ideas from urban ecology, the design sequence included five main steps: 1) Defining the system boundaries; 2) Analysing the system and its streams or flows – mainly calculating the metabolism of the system; 3) Finding and creating cyclifiers that could help in connecting the physical streams; 4) Developing cyclifiers on information and strategic layers; 5) Integrating the design to come up with a consistent whole.

To achieve a more connected, locally focused and sustainable city, the goal was a metabolic scheme of an almost completely looped system with several types of cyclifiers that can enable local food production, water purification, energy production and reuse

The design challenge was how to use design tools to map resources and urban flows and respond to the challenge of a shrinking city.

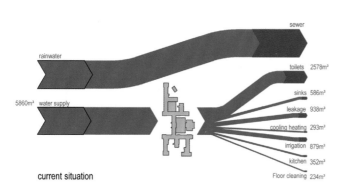

current situation

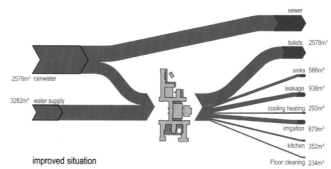

improved situation

2012Architecten, MSP2040 Urban Proposal, Heerlen, The
Netherlands, 2009
below: Recyclicity is used as a strategy to transform a mono-
functional district into a symbiotic community for living
and working. The systematic local short-cutting of currently
disconnected flows of food, energy, water and money is replaced by
an integrated and regenerative process.

bottom left: The leading intervention
is the transformation of the built and
paved environment into productive green.
A cyclifier is proposed, the Kaspaleis
(greenhouse plugin), which catches heat
loss from houses and makes it possible to
grow fruit and vegetables.

bottom right: Sankey diagrams for MSP2040. The calculated
streams show that all the water can be cleaned, stored on site and
used to water the crops, that most food can be produced within
the district's boundaries, that locally produced photovoltaic panels
can produce 60 per cent of the electricity needs, that greenhouses
can catch most of the heat loss from homes for growing food, and
that the growing local economy can allow the district to support
itself and cut itself loose from the social welfare its inhabitants are
currently dependent upon.

of building materials. This design sequence revealed that none of
the streams or flows, such as energy or materials, are integrated
on the site. For example, the data indicated that none of the food
produced on local farmland is processed on the site. Instead it
is transported elsewhere, processed, and transported back to the
supermarkets on site via another route. Cyclifiers are proposed
to allow most food to be produced and processed within local
boundaries, and all the water to be cleaned, stored and used on
site to water crops, with locally produced photovoltaic panels
contributing 60 per cent of the electricity needed for the area.

The results of the study are a good starting point for future
research, but issues such as time and method of data collection,
finding sufficient data for value calculations of the metabolism of
the systems and understanding the level of detail required for the
data were all major issues affecting the design of the cyclifiers. The
potential to reduce resource use from outside the local area is huge.

Future Developments

2012Architecten is currently working on integrating the
different data-collecting functions in an online tool that will help
analysis and modelling of the various data. New data leads to
new cyclifiers, and the revised results must then be checked and
new targets formulated. This iterative design cycle is what will
constantly improve the system. Many of the currently existing
tools are stand-alone, where data has to be transferred manually
between tables, maps, schemes and designs. 2012Architecten's
aim is thus to create a system modelling tool that acts as a
cyclifier for planning itself, linking strategies to knowledge and
interconnecting already present resources into an accessible design
mechanism. ⏃

Notes
1. See www.recyclicity.org.
2. Superuse was launched with a platform-based website, a book
and a film. See Ed van Hinte, Jan Jongert and Césare Peeren,
*Superuse: Constructing New Architecture By Shortcutting Material
Flows*, 010 Publishers (Rotterdam), 2007, www.superuse.org and
www.pbs.org/e2/episodes/306_super_use_trailer.html.
3. See www.cyclifier.org.
4. RB Fuller, 'Life/Syntropy/Entropy', *Intuition*, Doubleday (Garden
City, NY), 1972.

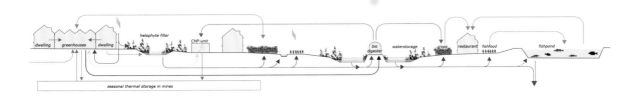

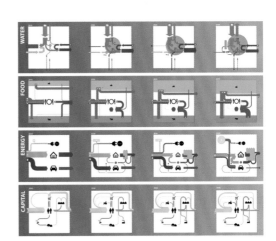

Nels Nelson, Symoto, Draft for online system modelling tool, 2011
Symoto (system modelling tool) is an online application for modelling systems and structuring data about consumption in cities so that one person can directly benefit from another's research. This allows users to quickly build a community of knowledge and information about how cities are performing with regards to water, energy, material and CO_2.

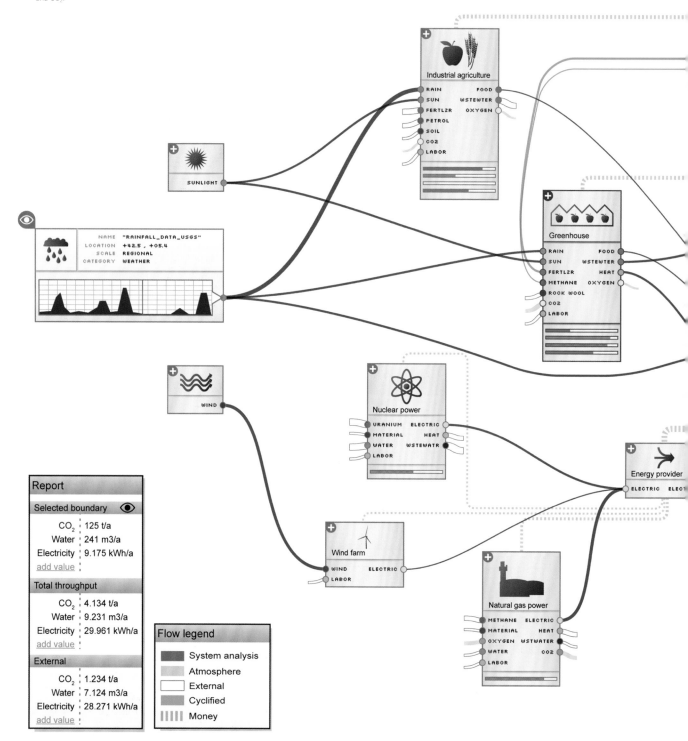

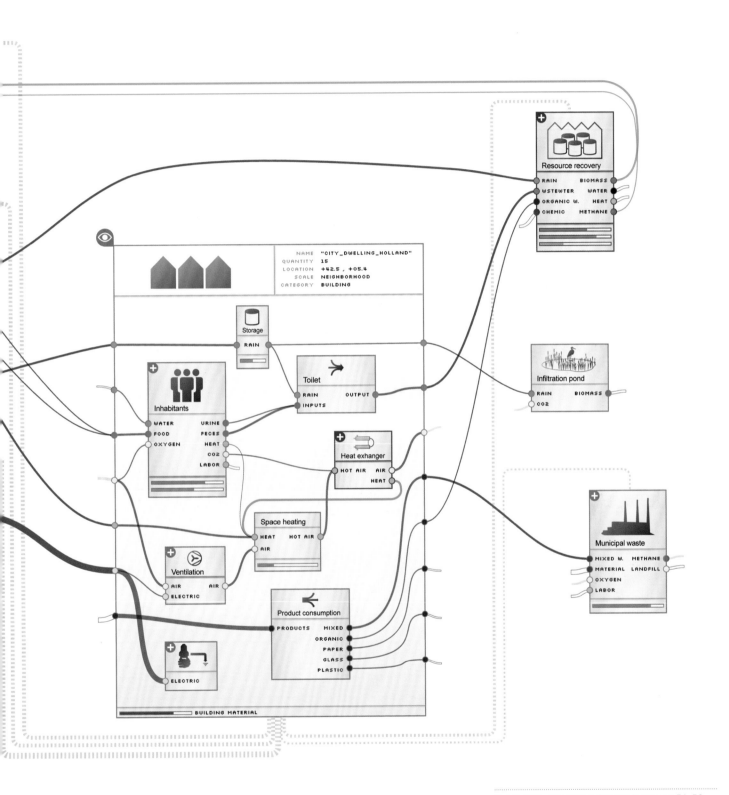

Simos Yannas

ADAPTIVE STRATEGIES FOR AN ECOLOGICAL ARCHITECTURE

Katerina Pantazi, Urban Rooftops, Athens, MArch Design Thesis,
Masters in Sustainable Environmental Design, AA School of
Architecture, London, 2010

Simos Yannas, Director of the Environment & Energy Studies Programme at the Architectural Association (AA) School of Architecture in London, calls for a rethink of architectural processes. Presently, architecture is conceived as an inanimate material system, but to become truly bioclimatic it needs to become adaptive in tune with the behaviour and the comfort of occupiers. Shifting from an emphasis on providing fixed interior conditions, it requires a dynamic approach to building performance and the resultant interactions between occupants, buildings and engineering appliances.

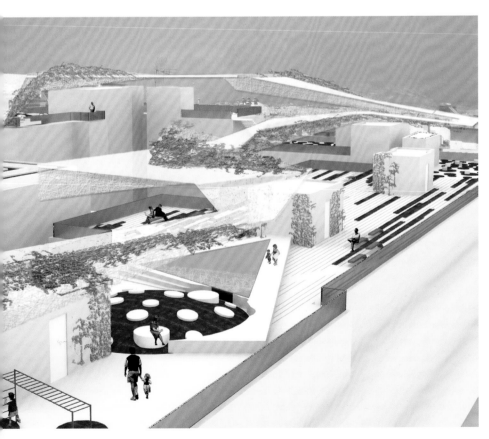

Ecological should be understood here as referring to processes and outcomes that are sustainable. As currently conceived and practised, architecture neither is, nor is meant to be, ecologically sustainable. Making architecture ecologically sustainable will require its inanimate materiality to become attuned to the variable biological clocks and activities of occupants inside, and to similarly variable natural rhythms and mundane activities outside.

Nitin Bansal, 'Corbu' in the Tropics, Chandigarh, MSc Dissertation,
Masters in Sustainable Environmental Design, AA School of
Architecture, London, 2009
right and below: The insights acquired from the study of on-site
measurements and from subsequent software calibration and
parametric studies introduce an entirely new dimension to the
understanding, appreciation and criticism of architecture and the
intentions of architects.

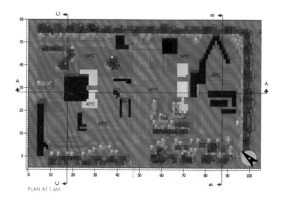

PLAN AT 1.6M

HIGH COURT, CHANDIGARH
Field Work: 1230hrs, 23th May, 2009

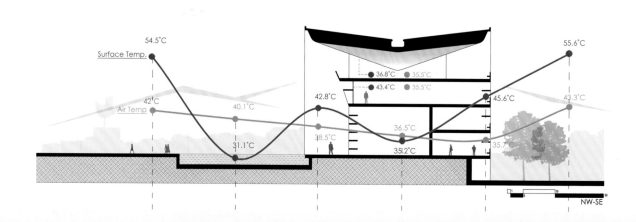

Attunement

To achieve such attunement, indoor spaces
and their constituent elements need to be
provided with the capacity to vary their
transmission of heat and light, and their
rate of air exchange with the outside. Doing
so selectively, for occupant comfort and
enjoyment, provides architecture with the
kind of adaptive mechanisms that can set it
free from conventional engineering systems.
Such adaptive mechanisms are at the core
of the bioclimatic approach in architecture, a
design paradigm that has gained mainstream
acceptance in recent years.[1] Which physical
properties of a building should vary, when,
where and by how much, for how long, on
whose command and with what activators?
These are key questions for research and
practice.

Mapping

From this viewpoint ecological research in
architecture must start by considering how
buildings are to be used; more specifically,
how the use of space might vary within and
between rooms, and over daily and seasonal
cycles, as well as following changes in
occupancy patterns and outdoor climate.
Unoccupied spaces have little, if any, need
for environmental servicing. On the other
hand, the presence and activities of occupants
create significant energy demands which vary
widely both within and between buildings.
The origins, frequency and intensities of
such energy demands characterise occupant
habits and expectations and thus also the
environmental profiles of different building
types and room functions. The mapping of
these patterns also highlights the spatial and
temporal distribution of internal heat

gains, the 'waste' heat energy released by
appliances, artificial lighting and occupants'
own metabolic processes.

Over the daily cycles, the rate of internal
heat generation can vary widely with
occupancy, but there is much less variation
seasonally. As a result, these heat sources
affect the energy balance of buildings all year
round, contributing to space heating and thus
saving energy in climates and buildings where
heating is needed, while causing overheating
and adding to cooling loads at other times or
in other climates. It follows that how densely
or sparsely spaces are to be occupied, the
nature of occupant activity and the time of
day and length of each occupied period are
critical variables with a profound effect on the
environmental performance of buildings and
on occupant comfort and enjoyment.

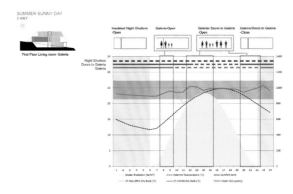

SUMMER SUNNY DAY
2 JULY

First Floor Living room- Galeria

Dana Bryan, Keunjoo Lee, Helene-Sophie Vlachos and Juliane Wolf, Housing at A Rocha Vella, Santiago de Compostela, Team Design Project, MArch Sustainable Environmental Design, AA School of Architecture, London, 2010–11
right, below and bottom: Rain (a dominant feature of the region's climate), wind, sun and occupancy patterns combine as form generators on this scheme to provide accommodation for an extended family on a semi-rural site on the outskirts of the city. Thermal simulations show that the building can achieve comfort conditions during occupied periods throughout the year without any need for mechanical heating or cooling.

① TRADITIONAL MASSING WITH DETACHED BARN

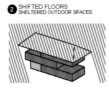

② SHIFTED FLOORS SHELTERED OUTDOOR SPACES

③ BENT PLAN INCREASED SOLAR ACCESS

④ WATER-HARVESTING ROOF SHEDS AND COLLECTS RAIN

⑤ SUN AND RAIN PROTECTION ADAPTABLE SCREENS

⑥ DORMERS AND WINDSCOOPS DIRECT AND DETER WIND SEASONALLY

Adaptation

Over the last century, the prevailing engineering view of thermal comfort had been that of a fixed neutral state that was to be maintained constant over predetermined periods by the operation of engineering appliances and their controls. By becoming dependent on non-renewable energy sources, this approach has proven to be extremely costly, yet rarely fully, if at all, satisfactory. Surveys have shown that far from viewing thermal comfort as a fixed or constant experience, occupants seek environmental diversity and achieve comfort through a dynamic process of physiological and behavioural adaptation.[2]

Supported with empirical data from field studies in different climates and building types, this adaptive approach to thermal comfort is now a feature of international standards.[3] At present this is in the form of simple empirical algorithms for determining lower and upper limits of thermal acceptability as a function of the outdoor temperature. As such, this has broadened the range of environmental conditions perceived as acceptable, allowing more accurate estimates of the heating and cooling loads of buildings, thus reducing the strain on conventional energy sources. It will take considerably more research for the various parameters involved to be characterised physiologically and behaviourally in a dynamic model for use as a design tool. Such a model would then also encompass those adaptive opportunities that architecture itself can provide its occupants, as discussed above.

Architecturing

Occupancy patterns and the expectations and adaptive behaviour of occupants determine the range of environmental conditions and functional requirements that translate into energy demands (for heating, cooling, lighting, appliances) in buildings. Climatic conditions outside a building may lessen or increase the intensity of such demands and may also introduce further design constraints and opportunities. Building form, spatial organisation and the internal and external properties of the building envelope are the means by which architectural design can meet or moderate occupant energy demands. Collectively these represent a vast combinatorial of historical precedents and potential future designs. While some of these variants have been studied empirically and/or analytically, the dynamic aspects of building performance and the resulting interactions between occupants, buildings and engineering appliances, are still poorly understood and largely unexplored architecturally. Simulation studies for different climates and building types show that optimising key design parameters for adaptive occupant and building behaviour can reduce space heating and cooling loads to insignificant levels thus drastically reducing the size and running costs of mechanical plant. Energy engineering can then come out of its closets in basements to become an integral constituent of the outer skin of buildings contributing to the supply of residual heat demands and electricity generation.

Katerina Pantazi, Urban Rooftops, Athens, MArch Design Thesis,
Masters in Sustainable Environmental Design, AA School of
Architecture, London, 2010
opposite, right and below: Studying the roofscape of residential
urban blocks in central Athens has highlighted considerable
potential for creating new recreational uses out of what are currently
wasted spaces. The geometry and microclimatic differentiations of
the rooftop environment suggest criteria for different activities.

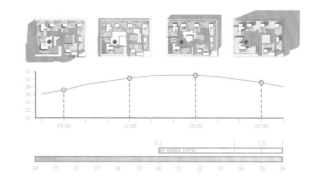

ENVIRONMENTAL
CONDITIONS

Air temperature
(typical summer day: 1st July)

EXPECTED
OCCUPANCY
PATTERNS

OCCUPANCY
ACTIVITIES/met

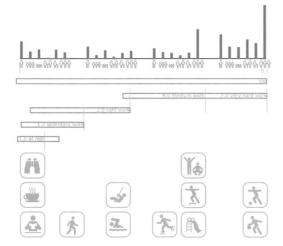

Symbiosis

A symbiotic relationship between buildings and the urban fabric they form and occupy is an essential condition for an ecological urbanism. By getting in the way of pre-existing energy flows, buildings alter the energy balance of their surroundings, fostering immediate microclimatic changes that affect them as well as impinging on other buildings and pedestrian activities in the vicinity. Equally importantly, buildings also engage in a continuous disposal of waste heat that they release to the urban environment outside by conduction, by air exchange and by the forced action of HVAC equipment. With these exchanges, each building acts like a giant heating system in the city. Whether in free-running mode or mechanically heated, ventilated or cooled, buildings will relentlessly warm the air around them, inducing complex longer-term effects that fragment the urban environment into a random assemblage of accidental microclimates which in turn subject the surrounding buildings to different environmental conditions than those for which they were originally designed.

Most cities have been experiencing localised climate change for a long time. There are now datasets[4] based on current climate change forecasts with which to predict the likely effects on energy demand and on occupant comfort indoors so as to assess design strategies for new buildings and refurbishment. However, while constructing alternative scenarios for large numbers of buildings is quite straightforward, predicting microclimatic conditions on any urban site is fraught with uncertainty, making designing in the urban context climatic guesswork. It is no wonder that so many buildings that had been hailed as low energy at the design stage ended up failing to deliver their predicted energy performance. Ultimately, it is the observation that the city both allows and fosters microclimatic diversity that gives the starting point for incremental urban cleansing and regeneration.

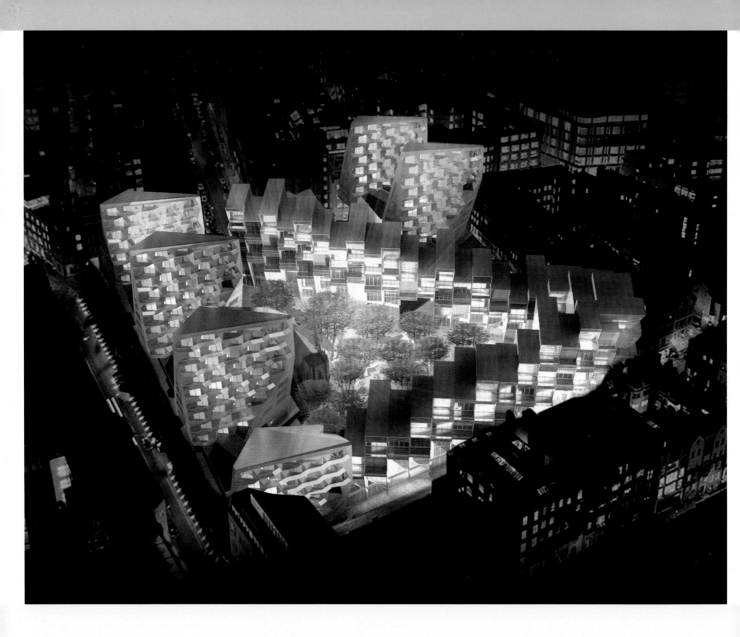

Education

These considerations and preoccupations are central to the Masters programme in Sustainable Environmental Design at the Architectural Association (AA) School of Architecture in London. Started in 1974, it has since grown into one of the largest programmes of its kind, with staff and graduates currently active in teaching, research and practice in some 50 countries. With an annual intake of up to 50 students from different countries, climates and cultural backgrounds, the main research object of the taught programme is the relationship between built form, materiality and environmental performance, and how this may evolve in cities in response to climate change and emerging technical capabilities. Fieldwork encompassing on-site observations and measurements, and use of computer modelling to simulate environmental performance and occupant comfort conditions, are essential learning techniques. These are introduced and practised from the beginning of the academic year on case studies of new and older buildings around London. Mapping the findings of on-site observations and measurements from these building studies informs on occupant behaviour and on building performance as well as serving to calibrate computer models that are then applied to run parametric studies with thermal, lighting and airflow simulation software. The findings of these studies become starting points for design research involving a variety of building types and climates.

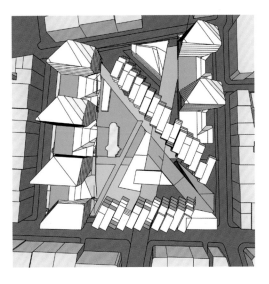

Herman Calleja, Noah Czech, Alexandre Hepner and Anna
Tziastoudi, Proposals for Mixed-Use Redevelopment of a Site in
Fitzrovia, London, Team Design Project, MSc/MArch Sustainable
Environmental Design, AA School of Architecture, London,
2010–11
opposite and left: Sun, wind and adaptive opportunities are the
generators for this urban scheme.

*Mapping the findings of on–site observations and
measurements from these building studies informs on
occupant behaviour and on building performance as
well as serving to calibrate computer models that are
then applied to run parametric studies with thermal,
lighting and airflow simulation software.*

Some of the programme's current
preoccupations and areas of research are
illustrated with the projects shown here,
and include learning from vernacular and
contemporary built precedents; housing
design and refurbishment in different
climates and urban contexts; occupant
thermal comfort and indoor environmental
quality as architectural concerns (rather than
engineering add-ons); the environmental role
of architectural design as arbiter of built form,
spatial organisation and material properties;
and parameters driving climate change in the
urban environment. ⌂

Notes
1. The term is attributed to Victor Olgyay who first used it for a paper
he wrote in 1953; it was subsequently popularised in his seminal
book *Design with Climate: Bioclimatic Approach to Architectural
Regionalism*, Princeton University Press (Princeton, NJ), 1963.
2. There is a large and growing literature on the adaptive model; for
a useful overview of current research see JF Nicol (ed), *Adaptive
Comfort, Special Issue of Building Research & Information*, Vol 39,
No 2, 2011.
3. See CEN Standard EN 15251, *Indoor Environmental Input
Parameters for Design and Assessment of Energy Performance of
Buildings Addressing Indoor Air Quality, Thermal Environment,
Lighting and Acoustics*, Comité Européen de Normalisation
(Brussels), 2007; see also American Society of Heating, Refrigeration
and Air-conditioning Engineers ASHRAE Standard 55-04, *Thermal
Environmental Conditions for Human Occupancy*, 2004.
4. The UK weather data with climate change scenarios are given
by the Chartered Institution of Building Services Engineers (CIBSE)
based on forecasts by the UK Met Office's Hadley CM3 Model. The
Meteonorm Global Meteorological Database (Meteotest, Bern 2009)
provides annual hourly datasets to the year 2100 for locations around
the world based on the same model.

Kasper
Guldager
Jørgensen

BUILDING NETWORKS FOR COLLA BORATIVE →

RESEARCH ON MATERIALS IN ARCHITECTURE

3XN, Microshade™ shading system, 2010
The Microshade™ shading system was developed as part of a collaboration between manufacturers Photosolar and the GXN studio with a research grant from the Danish Energy Agency. A solar shading system that can be integrated into facade glazing, it removes the need for external shading and reduces energy consumption in buildings with large glass facades. Microshade™ will be used on the facade of 3XN's Frederiksberg Courthouse, due to be completed in 2011.

3XN, GXN research studio, Copenhagen, 2007
In 2007, the GXN research studio was formed within 3XN to focus on green materials and technologies to inform and improve the architectural work of the office. Its four main areas of research are: 1) Informed design, which deals with integrated environmental information; 2) Technology design – embedded green-tech in building systems; 3) Experimental design – digital tools, complex geometry; 4) Material design – development and adaptation of materials.

3XN, Middelfart Savings Bank, Middelfart, Denmark, 2010
Middelfart Savings Bank has a dramatic roofscape accommodating multiple performance functions. The 83 prism-like skylights define the form of the roof and the geometry of the building, and frame the views to the sea.

3XN, Middelfart Savings Bank, Middelfart, Denmark, 2010
On-site installation of the 8-metre (26-foot) long roof elements using an efficient system based on precisely fabricated, off-site manufactured parts. This would normally have taken the contractor a month to install, but here was completed in only four days.

The roof openings bring in abundant amounts of daylight and allow for direct views of the sea from all areas of the building, and at the same time function as sun screening.

Kasper Guldager Jørgensen, Head of GXN at Danish practice 3XN, explains the vision behind the internal research group that investigates ecological design through digital processes and innovative material solutions. With a developed network of specialists, this relatively small group is able to draw on a much wider field of disciplines in its collaborations, whether it is working on an urban environmental project or contributing to materials studies with manufacturers and educational institutions.

In 2007, Copenhagen-based practice 3XN Architects established GXN, an internal research group with the mission to apply the latest knowledge and technologies to the field of architecture and design. The 'G' stands for Green, highlighting GXN's dedication to ecological design research through digital processes and innovative material solutions. The core goal is to develop a building culture that positively affects the world in which we live both architecturally and environmentally.

Networks for Material Innovation

GXN consists of eight architects, designers, researchers and engineers. This is a relatively large group compared to the size of the company, but very small if one considers the broad field of focus, which ranges from the application of parametric and scripted design tools to the adaptation of green materials and technologies. GXN is focused on the creation and maintenance of a strong professional network. Innovation often springs from the mixing and merging of expertise and experience from different fields, therefore all the office's

projects are created through interdisciplinary collaborations with selected specialists. For example, a current GXN research project is Urban Green, which aims to reintroduce nature and biodiversity into the built environment through a mapping of existing local environmental data.

The Urban Green project is a research collaboration with biologists, ornithologists, entomologists and chemists in which GXN, together with plant specialists 3kanten A/S in cooperation with Nissen Consult, is helping to develop designs for habitats which follow cradle-to-cradle principles that relate to the selection, breeding and production of wild plants from natural habitats. GXN sees potentials for these plants in the development of green walls and roof systems with the aim of improving air quality and highlighting water treatment potentials.

At the component scale, another example of collaborative design practice is in the development of an innovative architectural facade shading system. With fabricators PhotoSolar, and using the company's Microshade™ technology, GXN has received Danish Energy Agency funding for prototyping a new type of integrated window concept comprising sun screening, window and lamella. The result of the research is a shading system that will be used in the Frederiksberg Courthouse project by 3XN, which is currently under construction. Though the GXN team does not undertake core research on materials, it collaborates on studies with manufacturers, educational institutions, scientists, artists and other partners from the building industry.

How Research Informs Practice

A primary research question at GXN is how the development of design tools and adaptation of materials can serve as the basis for sustainable solutions. How can experimentation and research morph into practice? GXN undertakes some experimental, non-project-specific research in order to test ➔

3XN, Horten Law Offices, Copenhagen, 2009

below: A custom facade panel was specially developed for the Horten law offices, consisting of two layers of fibreglass composite with an insulating foam core, with an outer layer of travertine. At the research stage, several relevant references from ships and windmills were found – but no building projects with self-supporting and insulating fibreglass elements.

bottom: The first physical mock-up for the Horten law offices was inspected in Sweden. The facade was developed in collaboration with Pihl, Rambøll and Skandinaviska Glassystem.

opposite left: The anisotropic characteristic of the sandwich composite meant it was necessary to conduct thorough calculations of stresses in the fibreglass laminate.

opposite right: The sandwich composite used in the facade underwent rigorous testing to comply with the various regulations on everything from fire testing to adhesive ability.

Horten's exterior is designed in a three-dimensional geometric pattern that filters sunlight and promotes maximum daylighting.

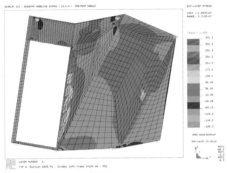

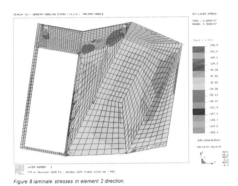

Figure 7 laminate stresses in element 1 direction.

Figure 8 laminate stresses in element 2 direction.

ideas. The Danzer Light project (2010), an installation created for an exhibition, uses the mathematical principle of aperiodic tiling to create a compact geometry. It consists of more than 100 pyramid-shaped elements, but only four individual components. All the elements have shared faces and can therefore be reconfigured in various combinations. The design is an example of how a complex design solution can be achieved through an understanding of smart geometrical principles – a feature that characterises the built work at 3XN, where three-dimensional facade elements can become ecological performance features due to built-in environmental behaviours. It demonstrates how GXN uses complex geometry and mathematical logic to achieve certain design qualities. Custom digital tools were developed using computer programming and scripting to understand the fractal and self-growing behaviour of the mathematical principles.

Some of these same strategies, such as spatial modularity and approaches for handling complexity, have also been used in building projects. For example, GXN developed the design for the three-dimensional roof of the Middelfart Savings Bank in Denmark (2010) by applying ongoing research into parametric design and geometry as it relates to environmental considerations. The roof consists of a large structure with 83 prism-like skylights that are designed to frame the view towards the water, while at the same time shading the building from direct sunlight. The modular design ensured an efficient installation process. A roof that normally would have taken the contractor a month to install was prefabricated and installed on site in only four days, saving energy and material. The money saved on installation was invested in quality materials and finishes.

The Horten headquarters project (2009), a new commercial building for a Danish law firm in Copenhagen, is another design by 3XN that aims to exceed the existing energy-performance regulations. Working with a similar shading strategy as that for the Middelfart Savings Bank, Horten's exterior is designed in a three-dimensional geometric pattern that filters sunlight and promotes maximum daylighting while providing each office with its own bay window and a view of the harbour. The shape of the building poses a 'closed' facade towards the south and an 'open' glazed facade towards the north. The building envelope protects against direct sunlight and excessive overheating. This results in significantly reduced energy consumption on top of stringent Danish building codes using national and international evaluating methods (LEED, BREEAM and DGNB).

In order to build the desired geometric shape, which was based on the site orientation and environmental data, GXN researched and designed new and innovative building materials and methods for the Horten project. The aim was to achieve a highly insulated, easy to install, composite panel that could exceed thermal performance. The solution is a lightweight sandwich panel facade system comprising two layers of fibreglass composite with a highly insulated foam core and a travertine cladding as the exterior finish. The result is a strong example of how a devoted research focus can lead to experimental and green facade solutions with materials innovation, inner spatial qualities and iconographic value. ∆

Laura Lesniewski

OMEGA CENTER
FOR SUSTAINABLE LIVING
LEARNING FROM NATURE

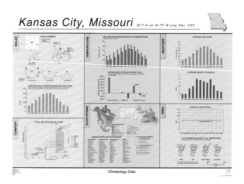

Kansas City, Missouri

Laura Lesniewski, Principal of BNIM, describes how Elements, an internal division of the US firm focused on sustainable design and research, made an essential contribution to BNIM's new facility for the Omega Institute for Holistic Studies in Rhinebeck, New York. Through the adoption of building information modelling (BIM) and other new tools and analysis techniques, and the optimisations of the three primary flows through the building – energy, air and water – it has realised a new standard in ecological design.

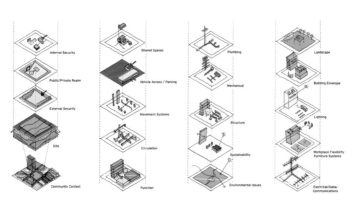

BNIM is an American design office of 60 architects, interior designers, landscape architects and planners. Established in 1970, BNIM is recognised as a pioneer in sustainable building, and in 2011 was awarded the AIA National Architecture Firm Award in recognition of its excellence in sustainable design. Elements is a division of BNIM focused on sustainable design and research, which also provides sustainability consulting services to the larger community.

In 2006, BNIM began work with the Omega Institute for Holistic Studies, an organisation designed to foster personal growth and social change, located in Rhinebeck, New York.[1] The brief was to design a new facility for the institute that would increase the capacity of Omega's on-site wastewater treatment (septic) system. The client also engaged Dr John Todd, a member of the Omega faculty who is a designer of wastewater treatment systems that use nature's principles to clean water with a healthy ecosystem, mimicking nature's estuaries.[2]

Early in the design process, BNIM used a design tool to record local environmental data. Its Climate Data Chart captures trends in annual precipitation, exact GPS coordinates to predict solar access both throughout a day and throughout the year, expected temperature and humidity conditions throughout the year, ecosystems and plant communities native to the area, annual wind patterns and characteristics. For Omega specifically, this research was augmented with a design team that included a botanist, hydrologist, water, civil and plumbing engineers and architectural and structural designers, as well as individuals from Omega who had decades of experience on the site and living within its climate. With these tools, the team prepared the design work to be replicable, high performing from an energy and water perspective, and to be inspirational to those that engage with it.

The Living Building Challenge[3] was used as a tool by the design and construction team to spur integrated design even further. Loose hand sketches were used to illustrate

BNIM Design Process
In an ideal project, the process is characterised by early research
and listening to clients and end users, as well as to nature. After
construction, user feedback and building system performance allow
a comprehensive effort of continuous improvement.

BNIM, Omega Center for Sustainable Living,
Rhinebeck, New York, 2009
Architectural sketches for the Omega Center helped test and
communicate early and detailed design ideas.

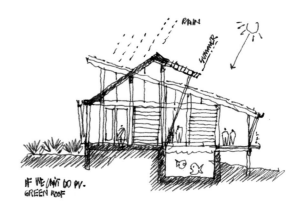

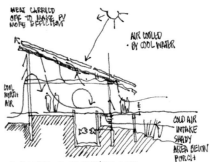

iterative design ideas, highly detailed lighting studies were
undertaken to minimise use of electric energy while still
providing adequate light for the plants in the Eco Machine
room and users of the classroom, and energy modelling
software was used to help balance solar access, solar shading,
natural ventilation strategies, thermal comfort and glazing
specifications. Building information modelling (BIM) was used
to ensure geometric integration of architectural, structural,
mechanical and plumbing systems. All water needed for
the Omega Center is captured on site and returned to the
groundwater after purification, all energy needed for the
building (on a net annual basis) is provided through on-site
renewable energy, and careful selection of materials creates
a healthy indoor environment where common toxins have
been minimised or eliminated altogether. In large dispersal
fields under the parking lot, the purified water is returned
to the aquifer beneath the campus. The design team took a
biomimetic approach with the rest of the facility, wrapping
the water treatment system with a building that similarly
embraced nature as a design teacher.

Ultimately, the design reflects optimisations of three
primary flows through the building: energy, air and water.
Daylight studies impact architectural form by dictating
large clerestories through which light enters. Structural
design affects thermal mass properties and therefore energy
performance, and the design of the wastewater system
impacts landscape architecture and vice versa, which in turn
refines the building form. All of this interaction requires design
dialogue and communication to be embedded in the culture of
all team members.

The team also used BIM to integrate architectural and
structural systems. In post-occupancy work, the office
collects and reviews various qualitative and quantitative
data, including anecdotes of the users, and actual water and
energy performance of the building systems. Only when this
information is gathered and measured can the implications

BNIM Evaluation Matrix Tool

below left: BNIM creates appropriate and highly graphic tools that help facilitate evaluation and decision-making exercises. This particular tool encourages clarity of thought and synthesis of ideas, while providing the project with a documented history of the research and ultimate decision.

BNIM, Omega Center for Sustainable Living, Rhinebeck, New York, 2009

below right: Annual daylight distribution. Lighting levels for each sensor were plotted for all 8,760 hours in the year to check for consistency in the 30,000-lux goal.

centre: Daylight simulation and optimisation. Several daylighting configurations were tested using the radiance-based simulation tool DAYSIM to optimise the amount of daylight at critical sensor locations for a typical cross-section close to 30,000 lux.

BNIM Sample Post-Occupancy Energy Analysis

bottom: So that the design team may continually look back and learn from design work, BNIM maintains ongoing analysis of actual energy performance as compared to design projections in design projects.

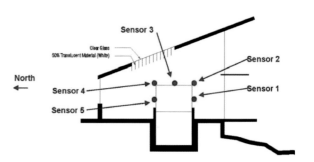

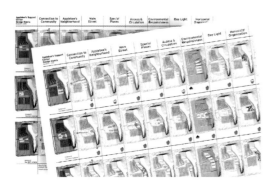

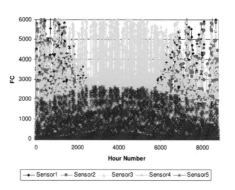

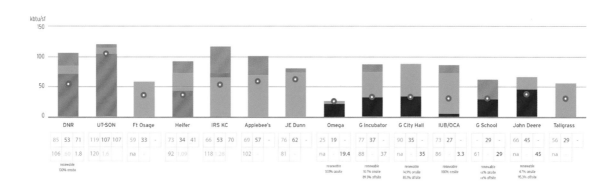

BNIM, Omega Center for Sustainable Living,
Rhinebeck, New York, 2009
left: The design of the self-sustaining, high-thermal mass building
emphasises daylight and natural materials and uses passive solar
heating supplemented by geothermal heating as needed, and
employs natural ventilation cooling strategies.

below: The Omega building is the only building in the world to
receive both LEED Platinum certification from the US Green
Building Council and certification as a Living Building.

of such a design process be known and learned to benefit future projects. As a signatory to the 2030 Challenge,[4] BNIM has documented design projects over the past few years to compare the work against various benchmarks, including regional benchmarks per building type via the US Environmental Protection Agency (EPA) Energy Star Target Finder tool, ASHRAE and LEED benchmarks, and the 2030 Challenge goals. By reviewing the progress of designs, and in some cases actual data from completed projects, BNIM is able to adjust design processes to ensure that lessons learned will beneficially impact the results of future buildings.

BNIM believes in the power of design to transform not only the built environment, but also the world. The office looks to nature to understand fundamental design principles, and its research into the ecology of a place informs its integrated approach to design. Its philosophy is thus centred on creating nature-inspired, generous architecture. ⌀

Notes
1. Pierre Teilhard de Chardin (1881–1955) was a French philosopher who conceived of the Omega Point, which is a state of maximum organised complexity.
2. Dr John Todd's Eco Machine™ design is an alternative method of treating wastewater that relies on understanding nature's principles. By allowing wastewater to filter through the roots of plants that are either suspended in indoor lagoons or planted in outdoor constructed wetlands, the micro-organisms that live in these habitats naturally and symbiotically treat our waste as food and ultimately clean the water. It is an approach that is readily scalable, from an individual scale to one that can treat water for an entire community.
3. The Living Building Challenge was first issued by the Cascadia Region Green Building Council and is currently monitored by the International Living Building Institute. The Omega Center project used Version 1.3 of the Challenge. Version 2.0 is available on the www. ilbi.org website.
4. Established by Architecture 2030 (www.architecture2030.org), the 2030 Challenge encourages the design community worldwide to adopt aggressive targets related to building performance, particularly as it relates to fossil fuel consumption, with an overall goal of achieving carbon-neutral designs (that is, no fossil fuel emissions to operate the building) by 2030.

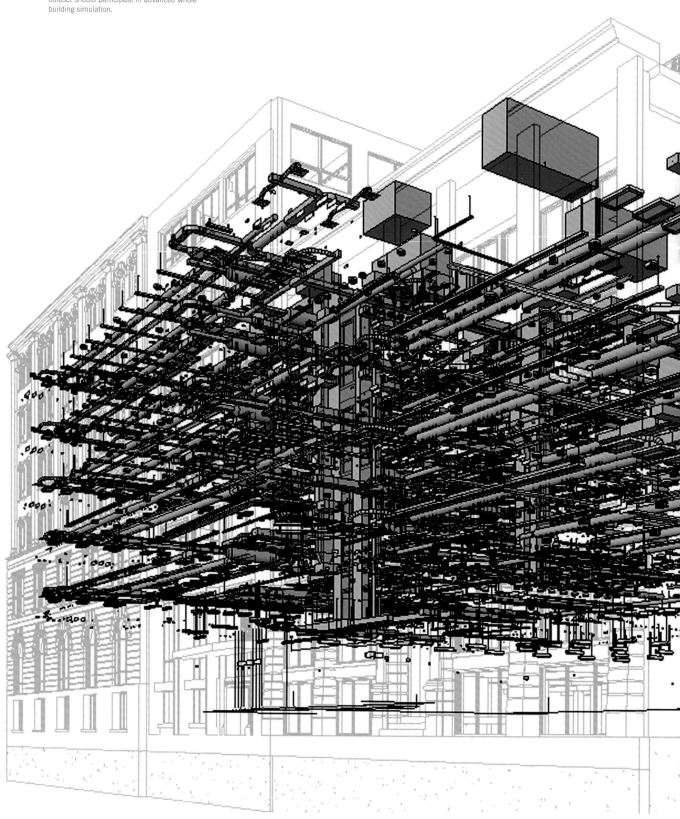

Andrew Marsh and Azam Khan

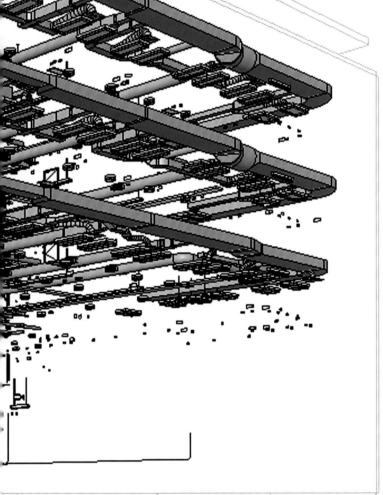

SIMULATION AND THE FUTURE OF DESIGN TOOLS FOR ECOLOGICAL RESEARCH

In sustainable terms, the complexity and inefficiencies of buildings present the most challenging environmental problem. Simulation remains the primary tool for the designer to develop intuitions and analysis of performance. **As Azam Khan, Head of the Environment & Ergonomics Research Group at Autodesk, and Andrew Marsh, Senior Principal Engineer at Autodesk,** explain, simulation can only be improved through the development of three key areas: more detailed modelling, building integration and by becoming indispensable to the design process.

Simulation is about complex relationships and time. Complexity can be defined in many ways, however, put

Christensen & Co Architects, Green Lighthouse, University of Copenhagen, Copenhagen, 2009
Diagram showing the design intent of the Green Lighthouse and its use of low-energy techniques such as natural ventilation and heating and cooling, and depicting occupants and environmental conditions.

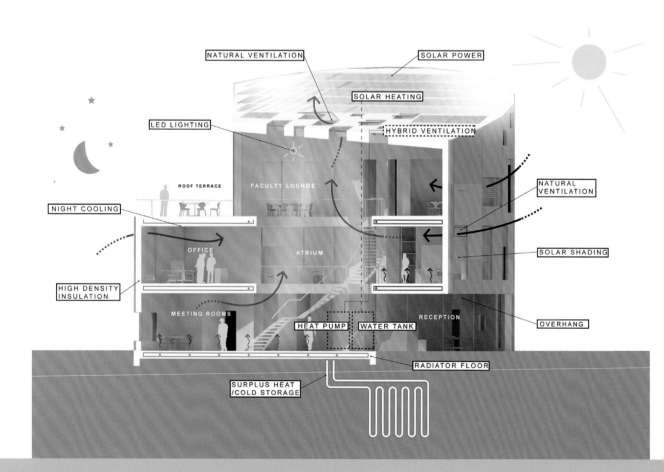

NATURAL VENTILATION   SOLAR POWER

SOLAR HEATING

LED LIGHTING   HYBRID VENTILATION

NATURAL VENTILATION

ROOF TERRACE   FACULTY LOUNGE

NIGHT COOLING

OFFICE   ATRIUM

SOLAR SHADING

HIGH DENSITY INSULATION

MEETING ROOMS   RECEPTION

OVERHANG

HEAT PUMP   WATER TANK

RADIATOR FLOOR

SURPLUS HEAT /COLD STORAGE

most simply it describes a system in which unspecified emergent behaviour can be observed.

As buildings mediate between a complex external system (weather) and a complex internal system (occupants), they are, themselves, bound to be complex systems with their own emergent behaviours. In his book *How Buildings Learn: What Happens After They're Built*,[1] Stewart Brand discusses buildings as responsive systems that acquire new 'knowledge' over time. This fits well with the human penchant for anthropomorphism, where we often see unpredictable response as 'character'. Also, just as with a biological organism, we see gradual degradation in use, usefulness, durability, performance and maintenance as 'ageing'.

Thus, when considering the countless interactions constantly occurring in a building, we see a strong mapping of architectural systems to ecological systems as temporal biotic members of an ecosystem. It is proposed here that, just like an ecosystem, when buildings work well with their environment they survive, but when they resist or fight their environment they do not.

Complexity and Efficiency

Complexity in nature has led to networks of interdependency that create essentially 'wasteless' systems. Given the relative scarcity of local resources in any environment, it is perhaps surprising that biological adaption has not optimised the operational efficiency of the individual parts of each system. In fact, the efficiency of many biological processes such as photosynthesis and digestion is actually quite low.[2] Instead, optimisation has occurred in the ability to collect and process waste generated by other parts of the system. At virtually every level, the production waste of one process is invariably of a form suitable as input for another. Even in death, biological organisms return their entire resources back to the local environment in a usable form.

In the pursuit of operational or structural efficiency, manmade complexity in manufacturing has often resulted in systems that create unusable or harmful emissions throughout the product life cycle, followed by total waste at the end of life. This life cycle is bracketed by unbalanced process efficiencies where, for example, automation has enabled the quick extraction of raw materials, production of artefacts and distribution to users. However, a notable lack of automation in the deconstruction and recapture of materials has resulted in a majority of used artefacts being treated as waste. Moreover, this waste is considered to be poorly differentiated and poorly separable primarily because automated deconstruction was not part of the original design process or intent.

Designed around the concept of the sundial, this building works with its environment using a self-shadowing entrance, copious skylights, solar panels, a natural ventilation stack effect, and automated smart lighting and exterior shades.

United Nations Environment Programme (UNEP), Diagram of
Environmental Impacts of Consumption and Production, 2010
The relative contribution to the total environmental problems caused
by material consumption is led by animal products (34.5 per cent),
crops (18.6 per cent) and coal (14.8 per cent), revealing gross
inefficiencies in building performance as buildings are the primary
cause of greenhouse gas production (48 per cent).

InterfaceFLOR, Balance of Automation in
Production and Consumption, LaGrange,
Georgia, 2008
right and opposite: InterfaceFLOR has
automated production and deconstruction,
turning fibre into fibre and backing into
backing, closing the carpet-recycling loop.

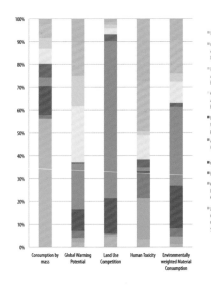

	Plastics
	Coal (Heating and electricity in housing)
	Natural Gas (Heating and electricity in housing)
	Crude Oil (Heating and electricity in housing)
	Biomass from forestry (Wood, paper and board)
	Animal Products (Animal protein and fish)
	Crops
	Iron and Steel
	Other Metals (Zinc, Lead, Nickel, Lead, Copper, Aluminium)
	Minerals (Glass, Salt, Concrete, Ceramics, Clay, Sand and Stone)

*We propose that buildings are the
predominant environmental problem
in the world because of complexity.
Buildings are irreducible systems with
massive emergent inefficiencies.*

Autodesk Research, Detailed architectural building information
model of 210 King Street, Toronto, 2010
Details need to be preserved for next-generation low-energy building
performance simulation.

A notable exception, where a factory and an 'unfactory' operate in parallel, is the ReEntry® 2.0 program at InterfaceFLOR. InterfaceFLOR is the world's largest carpet tile manufacturer with headquarters in Troup County, Georgia. Through ReEntry 2.0, InterfaceFLOR reclaims post-consumer vinyl-backed carpet – both Nylon 6 and Nylon 6,6. The backing is separated from the fibre and used to create material for new backing, while the fibre is recycled into new nylon for use by InterfaceFLOR and other industries.

Several metrics exist for understanding the imbalance between the production and consumption of resources. The Sustainable Consumption and Production Branch of the United Nations Environment Programme (UNEP) has proposed that an environmentally weighted material consumption value be formulated from three primary components including global warming potential, land use competition, and human toxicity.[3] UNEP reports that the relative contribution to the total environmental problems caused by material consumption is led by animal products (34.5 per cent), crops (18.6 per cent) and coal (14.8 per cent). The consumption of these animal and material products results in a combination of emissions and waste. Emissions can broadly be classified as air and water pollution. In particular, air pollution data from the US Energy Information Administration[4] and the United Nations Food and Agriculture Organization[5] report the three primary causes of the production of anthropogenic greenhouse gases (GHGs) to be buildings (48 per cent), the meat industry (18 per cent) and transportation (14 per cent). The inconsistency of these two sets of values indicates that buildings are incredibly inefficient with emissions greatly overshadowing those of animal products despite coal, used to generate electricity to power buildings, being less than half as harmful as the animal production industry.

It is thus proposed that buildings are the predominant environmental problem in the world because of complexity. Buildings are irreducible systems with massive emergent inefficiencies. While simulation is our primary tool to develop intuitions about the root causes of emergent behaviour, current tools have not had the impact on building performance that is needed to mitigate GHG production. There are several possible reasons for this. Perhaps simulation tools are perfect in every way but they are simply not being used. Perhaps the tools are not being used because they are not useful if they are used too late in the design process to make any difference. Perhaps they are too difficult to use or their output is not helpful. Maybe the problem comes later during construction where an efficient design is lost in translation, or during operation where efficiency declines rapidly. Perhaps the entire architectural design and construction process is itself an inefficient complex system.

The Future of Simulation

The future of simulation lies in three areas: more detailed modelling, building integration and becoming an indispensable part of any design process; that is, simulation as a design tool.

Modelling Detail

By definition, all simulation is based on some simplification of reality. The aim is to extract and model the most important relationships within a system while ignoring or factoring out those less important. In complex systems, determining which relationships are important is not always obvious. Neither is determining which inputs any particular relationship is dependent upon.

The problem in building simulation is that, often, analysis models are 'dumbed-down' due to limited available input data or in order for simulators to return results in a reasonable amount of time. For example, the specific usage patterns of a building are often factored out in favour of generic patterns common to building type. This completely removes the possibility of fully representing life-cycle events specific to that building. Clearly, this approach has not served us well.

The computerisation of the architectural design process has evolved over the last half century to the current state-of-the-art methodology of building information modelling (BIM). In parallel, in terms of operation, building management systems within completed buildings are proliferating and building automation systems have recently become the target of some computer networking companies. Also, with the advent of ubiquitous mobile computing and a greater awareness by the general public of inefficiencies in buildings, the demand to know what is going on in a building is steadily increasing.

Building information modelling and simulation (BIMS) could actually represent and report the level of detail needed, on an ongoing basis, to help make a building better and more useful over time.

Autodesk Research, Real-time visualisation of 210 King Street building information model, 2010
below: Autodesk's Project Dasher visualises real-time hierarchical energy-usage data, based on meters, sub-meters and sensors, at the 210 King Street office.

Autodesk Inc, Streamline visualisation of airflow simulation created in Autodesk CFDesign, 2011
bottom: Streamline visualisation of airflow simulation in a building showing transmission down stairs and over railing affecting occupants.

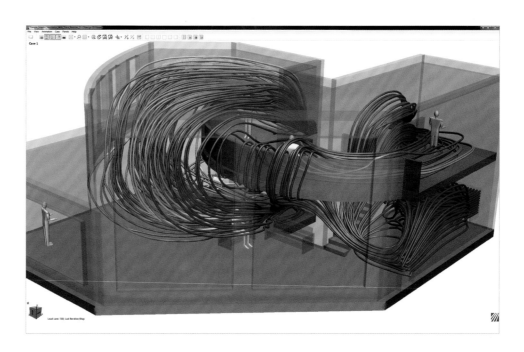

Fulfilling that demand means producing lots of information from within the building – sensing and monitoring energy use, room conditions, occupancy, solar radiation and a host of other real-time data. This will significantly impact simulation as it will enable building owners and occupiers to directly compare both predicted and measured performance. These kinds of comparisons are even becoming part of standard building regulations with the energy certification requirements of the EU Directive on the Energy Performance of Buildings.[6] To survive that comparison, simulators and software developers will need to make use of as much building-specific data as possible.

Perhaps, with the current stage of development of computer systems, we can attempt to 'smarten up' our models to include as much information as possible. Moreover, the 'smartening' process is already going on in the industry with BIM. Ideally, we could directly use this input for simulation without data reduction or remodelling. Building information modelling and simulation (BIMS) could actually represent and report the level of detail needed, on an ongoing basis, to help make a building better and more useful over time.

Building Integration

The next step for BIMS is to become an integral part of the building once it is completed. From the designer's point of view, simulated sensor values can be simply replaced by real sensor values when the building comes online. Just as commercial buildings today have a fire response sprinkler system, new and existing buildings could integrate a broader building response system (BRS).

In biomimicry terms, the key feature of this system would be resilience. It would include detailed instrumentation through sub-meters and sensors, real-time monitoring and analysis (via BIMS), as well as visualisation and reporting. Early implementations of a BRS could recommend building component optimisations, responding to real-time changes in power demand and local or remote generation. Intermediate systems could support real-time decision-making during emergency situations. Ultimately, advanced systems could learn and recommend design changes required to support continuous simulation as a design tool.

KPMB Architects, 210 King Street, East, Toronto, 1997 Renovation
The Autodesk offices in Toronto, an amalgamation of four heritage buildings, is the subject of Autodesk Research's Digital 210 King Project.

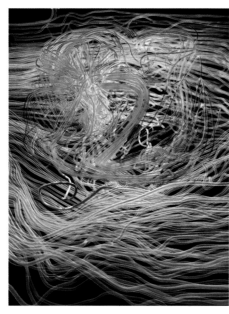

Autodesk Research, Renderings of flow
streamlines in Autodesk Maya, 2011
Visualisation experiments of streamline
geometry generated in Autodesk Maya
driven by Maya Fluids.

While the oversimplification of models is problematic, another critical limiting factor of today's simulation systems is interactivity. To serve as a useful tool throughout the design process, interactivity is needed to support playful iteration and 'optioneering' – the continuous testing of multiple design options. When system response times fall below a small threshold, users typically have difficulty maintaining context, and the tool loses its usefulness within the design process. The very motivation for reducing models down to their most basic components was to increase computational performance. Still, even with 'dumbed down' tools, the current generation of architects and building designers will have the most detailed knowledge and understanding of building performance of any time in history. Using analysis and simulation techniques, it is possible to model and test the performance of a huge range of design options in a very short amount of time, something that only a generation ago would have taken a lifetime's worth of observation and empirical experience to acquire. Smarter and more interactive models will only enhance this process.

This leads to another avenue for building simulation research and development, namely the adoption of high-performance computing techniques. The most common simulators used today are based on patterns created in decades long past as monolithic systems. This presents significant obstacles for these systems to take advantage of modern technologies. However, imagine interactive fluid dynamics simulations supporting real-time flow design for natural ventilation.

Autodesk Research envisions a new extensible collaborative interactive simulation framework and, to this end, has founded the Symposium on Simulation for Architecture and Urban Design (SimAUD).[7] The purpose of SimAUD is to support a new and ongoing dialogue between the simulation research community and the architecture research community. Admittedly, this is not a small task and the efforts of the broader building science community and others will be needed to develop a compelling system.

In summary, integrated real time lifecycle simulation could be a powerful tool supporting early conceptual design, continuous improvement and automated deconstruction. While this may represent a paradigm shift across several related industries, it may be a critical component for global progress in sustainability. ∆

Notes
1. S Brand, *How Buildings Learn: What Happens After They're Built*, Penguin (New York), 1995.
2. D Hall and K Rao, *Photosynthesis*, Cambridge University Press (Cambridge), 1999.
3. E Hertwich, E van der Voet, S Suh, A Tukker, M Huijbregts, P Kazmierczyk, M Lenzen, J McNeely and Y Moriguchi, *Assessing the Environmental Impacts of Consumption and Production: Priority Products and Materials*, A Report of the Working Group on the Environmental Impacts of Products and Materials to the International Panel for Sustainable Resource Management, United Nations Environment Programme (Paris), 2010.
4. US Energy Information Administration, *Assumptions to the Annual Energy Outlook*, US Energy Information Administration (Washington DC), 2008.
5. H Steinfeld, P Gerber, T Wassenaar, V Castel, M Rosales and C de Haan, *Livestock's Long Shadow: Environmental Issues and Options*, Food and Agriculture Organization of the United Nations (Rome), 2006.
6. *Energy Performance of Buildings (Certificates and Inspections) (England and Wales) Regulations 2007*, The Stationery Office (London), 2007.
7. R Attar (ed), *SimAUD 2011: Proceedings of the Symposium on Simulation for Architecture and Urban Design*, Society for Modeling & Simulation International (Boston, MA), 2011.

Perkins+Will Canada, Brighouse Elementary School, Richmond, British Columbia, 2011
The Richmond school district has identified the Brighouse Elementary School project as an opportunity to promote sustainability as a teaching tool.

*Peter Busby, Max Richter
and Michael Driedger*

TOWARDS A NEW RELATIONSHIP
WITH NATURE
RESEARCH AND REGENERATIVE
DESIGN IN ARCHITECTURE

The Living with Lakes Centre is designed for a 2050 climate. Situated at the centre of more than a million lakes of the Boreal Shield ecozone, Sudbury is an ideal location for the construction of a regenerative building.

Here **Peter Busby, Michael Driedger and Max Richter of Perkins+Will Canada (P+W)** describe the office's core focus on 'regenerative design': an approach where each operation in a building's construction is measured by its positive impact on human and natural systems. This is supported by an in-house research team of architects, engineers and sustainability strategists that concentrates on the advancement of sustainable building practices. They describe how this is played out in projects such as the Living with Lakes Centre at Laurentian University in Sudbury and the VanDusen Botanical Garden Visitor Centre, Vancouver.

Perkins+Will Canada (P+W) is an integrated architecture, interiors and planning firm and a North American leader in the field of sustainable design research.[1] Applying research to design challenges is an essential foundation of the firm's methodology. The Vancouver office's in-house research team includes architects, engineers and sustainability strategists and focuses on the advancement of sustainable building practices.[2] It leads independent research work and assists project teams in areas such as evaluating the sustainability of materials, developing strategies to reduce glare, investigating the carbon impacts of forestry practices and timber construction, evaluating green building rating systems and developing design processes that integrate energy modelling into decision-making matrices. It provides internal advice on sustainable building features, systems, and the wide variety of benefits derived from pursuing green building initiatives. The P+W office collaborates with research institutes from universities across North America to advance its understanding of critical ecological issues.

P+W's core practice is based on an environmental strategy of 'regenerative design'.[3] The office defines this as a design approach where each act of construction and operation of buildings and communities has a positive effect on the systems it affects. Its aim is to positively influence human and natural systems by bringing them into integration. Each project is evaluated on the basis of the metrics of energy usage intensity, carbon usage intensity, water usage intensity, avoidance of chemicals of concern and third-party green rating certification. The P+W research team is involved with the development of the metrics and with tracking project performance.

Living with Lakes

An example of the regenerative design approach is the Living with Lakes Centre for Applied Research in Environmental Restoration and Sustainability project completed in 2011 at Laurentian University in Sudbury, Ontario. The project design focuses on improving the environmental context through the construction and occupancy of a building. The surroundings include Lake Ramsey, the city's drinking water reservoir and an important centre for the Canadian mining industries. The emissions from the smelters and other industrial activity in the region have caused extensive ecological damage to lakes and ecosystems.

In 2006, P+W began the design of new research facilities at Laurentian drawing on the knowledge of the university's internationally recognised researchers and scientists.

Perkins+Will Canada, VanDusen Botanical Garden Visitor Centre, Vancouver, 2011
The Glulam roof panels for VanDusen were prefabricated approximately 40 kilometres (25 miles) away and installed on site.

Laurentian's scientists have expertise in protecting and restoring damaged ecosystems, and worked with the P+W design team to create a facility that not only minimises its ecological footprint, but also assists in the restoration of the local ecosystem. The project includes 488 square metres (5,253 square feet) of open area research wet lab as well as a research facility dedicated to the sustainability of watersheds. The design allows the building to function as a restorative insertion within the landscape. Manitoulin Island limestone, an alkaline material, is used for the building and the landscaping so that stormwater running off site will assist in neutralising the acid by-product of the smelting processes taking place in the area.

The P+W research team also worked with climate scientists at the University of British Columbia (UBC) in Vancouver to develop a set of design objectives for the project. Design features for both energy and water conservation include: green roofs to reduce stormwater runoff; a high-performance thermal envelope analysed through LEED-compliant energy modelling; a ground source heat pump; hydronic radiant floor heating; passive heating and cooling; solar domestic water heating; storm- and greywater treatment; permeable paving for driveways and parking lots; natural daylighting studies; energy-efficient lighting and appliances; building automation systems; and use of natural and local materials.

VanDusen Botanical Garden Visitor Centre
Selection of appropriate materials is one aspect of sustainable design on which architects have a significant influence, yet some of the most ecologically problematic substances are used in building materials. In 2002 the P+W office began work on a cancer centre and set about tracking down all known carcinogens in building products. Following on from this research, they developed the Precautionary List – a list of 25 substances that are of concern to human or environmental wellbeing – and in 2007, with researchers at Yale University, began further investigations into a number of these substances and their effects on ecological systems.

P+W's Precautionary List is now a public document, available online,[4] that is used by the firm's architects, designers and the general public to identify human and

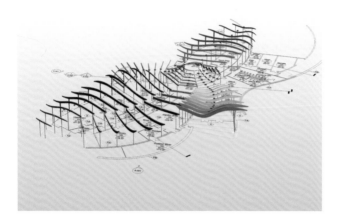

Roof petals around the visitor centre oculus establish the building's form.

East view of the centre showing the green roof, solar panels and rammed-earth walls.

environmental health concerns, and gives researchers and academics a better understanding of the substances in common building components. The list was used to inform material selection for P+W's new visitor centre at the VanDusen Botanical Garden in Vancouver (2011), for which the design and research teams worked closely through the design and construction phases to choose building materials that would qualify the project for certification under the Living Building Challenge rating system.[5]

Precaution as a design strategy was most fully tested in the VanDusen project. One of the biggest obstacles to avoiding the use of building materials on the Precautionary List is the lack of public information about what goes into them. To prevent the accidental inclusion of such materials, building materials and components that are easy to identify and contain minimum 'ingredients' were used so that the material resources embodied in the project could be captured and reused at the end of the project life cycle, as well as to simplify building maintenance. The simple material palette does not compete visually with the flowing, organic spaces of the building, but enhances the building's natural garden setting.

Wood was chosen as the primary structural material for the visitor centre. Lumber that is sustainably harvested and well protected within the building envelope can provide an important ecological function, storing carbon dioxide throughout the life of the building. For Living Building Challenge certification, the project is required to document and offset the carbon emissions related to the building material production and extraction as well as the construction of the building and landscape. Wood presents two important advantages to this carbon accounting: it is local, and the carbon emissions from sustainably harvested lumber are lower than that of other structural material options.

The visitor centre was the first project on which the P+W team collaborated with an ecologist to inform the design of both the building and the systems that affect its energy, water and environmental performance. Ecologists look beyond property lines to how plants and animals interact with the building and surrounding ecosystem services. This holistic perspective enabled the design team to focus on larger-scale water usage and ecological factors to influence both building and landscape design, a strategy that was later also used for the firm's Earth Science Building at UBC (due for completion late 2012) and Brighouse Elementary School in Richmond, British Columbia (2011). At Brighouse, the results of such collaboration include restorative landscape features that account for bird migration and insect migration (butterflies); thus the school acts as a learning tool for the students as well as responding to the context of the site prior to development, extending the factors that influence design beyond the boundaries of the building.

Collaboration with academic institutions, ecologists and a dedicated research team results in design decisions that are best suited to a project's site conditions for more holistic design solutions. By looking beyond conventional design, buildings can serve as living laboratories while also addressing issues beyond their site boundaries. This overall shift in P+W's design approach has led to the firm's most innovative and sustainable projects to date. ⌂

Ecologists look beyond property lines to how plants and animals interact with the building and surrounding ecosystem services. This holistic perspective enabled the design team to focus on larger-scale water usage and ecological factors to influence both building and landscape design

Notes

1. Perkins+Will Canada defines 'sustainable design' as design that achieves a balance between the positive and negative impacts of buildings and development.

2. Examples of the internal research work are available on the P+W Canada website: www.perkinswill.com/purpose/innovation.html.

3. Regenerative design is an approach to design where each act of construction and operation of our buildings and communities has a positive effect on the systems it affects. While sustainable design seeks to create balance between the positive and negative impacts of buildings and development, regenerative design seeks to positively influence human and natural systems by bringing them into integration.

4. The Precautionary List can be found at http://transparency.perkinswill.com/.

5. The Living Building Challenge (LBC) is a rating for sustainable building and community development projects, introduced in 2006 by the Cascadia Region Green Building Council. See www.ilbi.org.

Regenerative design solutions at campus level. The CIRS exchanges heat with a neighbouring building, lowering the energy consumption and carbon footprint of the campus.

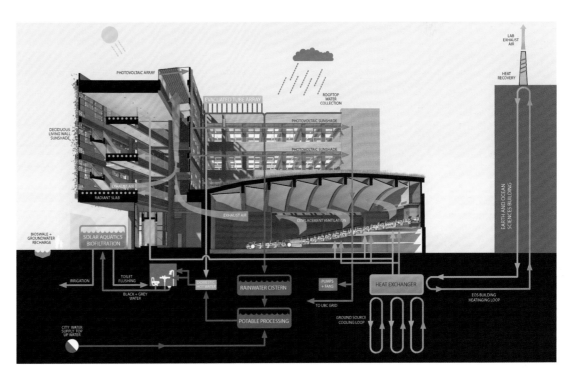

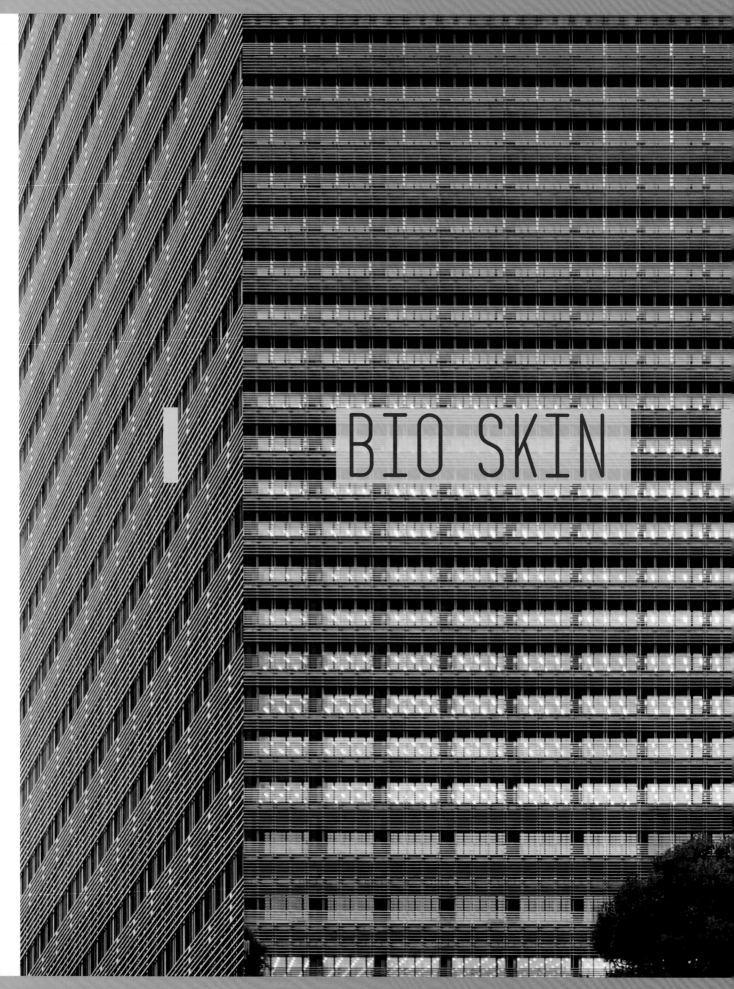

BIO SKIN

URBAN COOLING FACADE

Tomohiko Yamanashi,
Tatsuya Hatori, Yoshito
Ishihara and Norihisa
Kawashima (Nikken
Sekkei Ltd) and Katsumi
Niwa (Nikken Sekkei
Research Institute)

Nikken Sekkei, Sony Research and
Development Center, Tokyo, 2011
Nikken Sekkei's new research and development
headquarters for Sony is clad in a new facade
system called BIO SKIN, which is the result
of ongoing research into the urban heat island
phenomenon by the Nikken Sekkei Research
Institute (NSRI).

Numbering 65, Nikken Sekkei's research group is the size of many substantial practices. **Tomohiko Yamanashi, Tatsuya Hatori, Yoshito Ishihara and Norihisa Kawashima at Nikken Sekkei Ltd and Katsumi Niwa at the Nikken Sekkei Research Institute (NSRI)** describe the unique collaborative processes that make the NSRI's contribution essential to any Nikken projects requiring the development of cutting-edge technology or urban planning proposals. Here, they detail the development of BIO SKIN, an innovative facade system developed for the Sony Research and Development Center in Tokyo, which addresses the urban heat island effect, one of the main environmental research areas of the NSRI.

Nikken Sekkei is one of the world's largest architectural design firms with over 2,500 professional staff. Established in 1900, from its headquarters in Tokyo it offers comprehensive design, engineering, management, consulting, and research and development (R&D) services for the built environment. Nikken Sekkei Research Institute (NSRI) was established in 2006 as a separate entity within the Nikken Group, as a think tank providing R&D consultation relating to sustainable urban design. NSRI employs 65 personnel including urban planners, energy consultants, consulting engineers, architects and researchers. It is an influential and unique research group within Japan and has consulted on many of Nikken Sekkei's 20,000 building and urban planning projects worldwide. NSRI's research is based on the themes of city administration, environment and energy with the goal of unifying value creation, environmental load reduction and appropriate evaluation for more effective city management.

NSRI collaborates on Nikken projects requiring the development of cutting-edge technology, and on all urban planning proposals. Through daily communication, its researchers determine what the design teams require from the NSRI, and propose design tools and technologies for urban design at all scales, including the human scale, collaborating at various project stages with Nikken Sekkei architects and urban planners. Such integration is what makes the Nikken Group different from other firms. At the beginning of a project, the NSRI collaborates in the making of a 'road map' where many related disciplines join together. Following this, the various disciplines and specialists are involved in targeted ways depending on the specific needs of the project.

In March 2011, Nikken Sekkei architects completed a new research and development office for Sony. Located near the West Gate of Osaki Station in Shinagawa City, Tokyo, the building is clad in an innovative facade system called BIO SKIN, which was developed by Nikken Sekkei with several partners including the NSRI. BIO SKIN was designed to reduce both the heat load inside the building and the urban heat island effect, one of the main environmental research areas of the NSRI. Specifically, it functions as a handrail of the balcony on the northeast facade of the building and as a sunshade during the morning hours. Thanks to its efficacy in evaporative cooling, it helps reduce the temperature in the surrounding areas. This strategy of mitigating the urban heat island effect was a main performance driver of the project. Tokyo has been experiencing a serious urban heat island phenomenon in recent years, which triggers occasional unexpected heavy rain called 'guerrilla rain'.

The design team included NSRI, landscape designers and other consultants who studied various design options using bespoke digital tools for thermal environmental simulation. While an increase in the amount of vegetation is proven effective in reducing the heat island effect, the site of the new building is such that the main facade would face northeast, making it unfavourable to design a wall covered with vegetation. In addition, there was limited space to add planting around the building. The planning team strived to create a significant environmental effect, similar to that of tree canopies, to shade the building. The planners were also inspired by the traditional Japanese cooling method of sprinkling water around a house in the summer. A system was developed to evaporate the rainwater from inside porous ceramic tubes on the exterior surface of the building. To meet the various design challenges, Nikken Sekkei needed to collaborate with manufacturers and research institutions from an early stage. The team studied a wide range of issues from the micro to the urban scale.

The first work undertaken was a series of mock-up experiments of BIO SKIN materials. The design team used porous terracotta which is suitable for evaporation of internal moisture. Performance was compared by installing sample

left: View from Osaki Station showing the BIO SKIN facade system. The system was inspired by the traditional *uchimizu* summer water ritual in which water is sprinkled on the ground and gardens to cool the air.

above: The entire east side of the Sony building is clad in the new BIO SKIN louvre system which draws heat energy from the surrounding environment as it evaporates, reducing the surrounding air temperature by 2°C (3.6°F).

above: View of the east facade showing the BIO SKIN system of
high-porosity ceramic pipes that circulates water within the facade.

opposite bottom (right): The BIO SKIN louvres are inspired by traditional *sudare*, decorative screens or blinds used to shade openings of buildings from light and heat.

opposite top and right: The *screen*-like design of BIO SKIN allows views out across the city.

Environmental measuring sensors monitor the performance of the BIO SKIN facade.

ouvres made from terracotta, which have a high evaporative cooling capacity, alongside ordinary sample louvres made of aluminium. These were installed to face the same direction as the actual proposed building plan, and their surface temperature, ambient temperature, amount of evaporation, temperature and humidity of the surrounding areas, and wind speed were measured at periodic intervals. The temperature of the wet terracotta louvre was 5 to 6°C (9 to 10.8°F) lower than that of the aluminium louvre, proving the superior cooling capacity of terracotta. In addition, the experiment provided evidence of the correlation between the surface temperature and amount of evaporation with the external environment.

The results of the mock-ups and other studies, such as airflow analysis, confirmed the air-cooling effects of the louvres made of wet terracotta. The numerical simulation, based on the measured data, indicated that the BIO SKIN's surface temperature could be 10°C (18°F) lower on the hottest day in the summer, while the airflow analysis showed that the BIO SKIN wall could help reduce the temperature in the surrounding walkways and the entrance hall by 2°C (3.6°F). Temperature near the glass surface of the exterior wall equipped with BIO SKIN is also 1 to 2°C (1.8 to 3.6°F) lower at each floor, proving the effect of reducing the use of air conditioning in the summer. The design team concluded that the resultant 2°C (3.6°F) reduction in the surrounding temperature should be a feasible target, given the fact that the heat island effect has raised Tokyo's annual average temperature by 3°C (5.4°F), which is 2°C (3.6°F) higher than the rise of only 1°C (1.8°F) in other cities.

Mould and moss tend to grow on terracotta due to its high water absorption rate. This problem has been resolved by a photocatalytic coating of titanium oxide (TiO_2) on the terracotta louvres and by installing them with sufficient air gaps in a well-ventilated area. The high water absorption rate also can cause ice jams in the winter. Shaping the louvre symmetrically with a certain thickness helps disperse the expansion and contraction stress caused by freezing water. The extrusion moulding process tends to make the material's surface dense and cause clogging, and this design problem was addressed in the manufacturing process.

The BIO SKIN uses rainwater that is collected from the roof, stored in the basement storage tank, filtered, pumped up, and supplied to the BIO SKIN of each floor. Clean water can also be used in the event that continuous clear days result in a shortage of rainwater. The design team also installed environmental measuring sensors to create a system that allows monitoring of the cooling effect of the building energy management system.

A tension structure has been used so that the BIO SKIN is supported with minimal components. The tension rods can absorb tensile force of over 3 tons, with due consideration in temperature change. Use of extremely thin rods prevents obstruction of vision, giving a consistently cool and light appearance.

The BIO SKIN project was undertaken by the design team using a Japanese-style integrated project delivery (IPD). In designing the components necessary to realise the new high-performance architecture, Nikken Sekkei developed the requisite new technology jointly with several manufacturers who, as the result of a competitive process, excelled in controlling performance and costs. This procedure was one of the reasons behind the successful adoption and realisation of the new technology. Another was collaboration with a number of university research institutions, which enabled the design team to develop the technology through simulation-based research and the use of the quantitative data. ◖

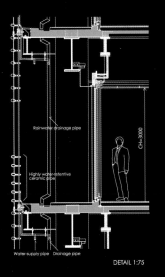

Rainwater drainage pipe

Highly water-retentive ceramic pipe

CH=3000

Water-supply pipe   Drainage pipe

DETAIL 1:75

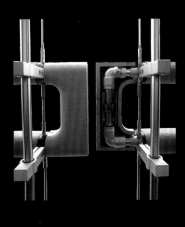

JOINT DETAIL

Joint Detail

The design considers water use and distribution across the entire site. Excess water is impregnated in the soil as much as possible to allow normalisation of the water cycle and reduction of load in the sewage infrastructure of the urban environment.

Outer surface (shot-blasted)

Inner surface

×5000   ×1000   ×500

PHOTOMICROGRAPH

Core material: Aluminum extruded material   Elastic adhesive   Highly water-retentive terra-cotta louver

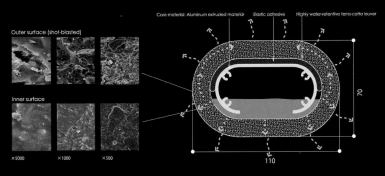

70

110

LOUVER SECTION

Louvre Section

By cooling prevailing winds from the south that strike the side of the building facing east, the temperature of the surrounding air can be reduced by 2˚C (3.6˚F).

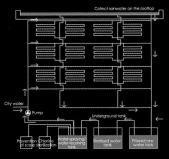

Collect rainwater on the rooftop

City water

Pump

Underground tank

Prevention of scale   Chlorine sterilization   Water-spraying/water-receiving tank   Sterilized water tank   Filtered raw water tank

WATER CYCLE IN THE BUILDING

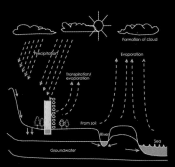

Formation of cloud

Precipitation

Transpiration/evaporation

Evaporation

From soil

River

Sea

Groundwater

WATER CYCLE IN THE CITY

Water Diagram

Rainwater is collected from the rooftop and stored in underground storage tanks before being pumped up and circulated through the pipes in the facade. The rainwater penetrates the porous ceramic and then evaporates from the pipe surface thereby cooling the surrounding air.

Text © 2011 John Wiley & Sons Ltd. Images: pp 100–01, 103–05 © Harunori Noda (Gankohsha); p 102 © Yutaka Suzuki/HybridStudio; p 107 © Nikken Sekkei Ltd (SEO Kazuhiro Otaka)

**Atelier Ten, Grant Associates and Wilkinson
Eyre, Gardens by the Bay, Bay South,
Singapore, 2011**
Arrivals cluster Supertrees. The Supertrees are
manmade concrete and steel structures that
incorporate vertical gardens, elements of the
building services and energy harvesting systems
(such as the photovoltaic panels pictured) and a
bar in the tallest Supertree.

GARDENS BY THE BAY
ECOLOGICALLY REFLECTIVE DESIGN

Meredith Davey of Atelier Ten describes how as part of a design team led by Grant Associates with architects Wilkinson Eyre, multidisciplinary engineers Atelier Ten have developed a scheme for the Gardens by the Bay, Bay South in Singapore based on first principles. Holistically integrated solutions have been sought to the central and demanding brief to create artificial interior environments that will enable Mediterranean and mountain plants to grow in the tropical urban heat of downtown Singapore.

Atelier Ten is an innovative multidisciplinary firm of building services engineers, environmental design consultants and lighting designers focused on delivering high-quality building services design and sustainable design consultancy within the planned and built environment. The office engages in a macro-to-micro approach to planning and design, always concentrated on making the most of environmental opportunities and enhancing the human experience in its projects. Founded in 1990, Atelier Ten has offices in London, Glasgow, New York, New Haven and San Francisco.

The Gardens by the Bay, Bay South project was commissioned via an international competition by the National Parks Board of Singapore (NParks) in 2006. The competition was won by a team led by Andrew Grant of Grant Associates and included architects Wilkinson Eyre with engineering by Atelier One (structural, with local support from Meinhardt) and Atelier Ten (building services and environmental) with local support from CPG Consultants.

top: Architectural renderings of the Flower Dome (left) and Cloud Forest (right) biomes with the hub (centre). The conservatories use an automated external shading system to manage the daylight levels inside the space for optimal horticultural needs.

right: Conceptual layering of the Supertrees and conservatories. Purple lines represent flows of air or water in subterranean networks connecting the Supertrees, conservatories and energy centre.

Atelier Ten acted as the environmental and sustainable design consultant and building services engineer, working with locally based CPG Consultants through the delivery phase. The Bay South project comprises 52 hectares (128 acres) of landscaped gardens on reclaimed ground in Singapore's new downtown in Marina Bay. It features a 20,000-square-metre (215,278-square-foot) complex of cooled conservatories and 18 huge structures supporting vertical gardens ranging in height from 25 metres (82 feet) to 50 metres (164 feet), known as the Supertrees.

The project developed a significant number of non-conventional design constraints and design responses due to the central brief to create artificial interior environments, to allow cool Mediterranean and tropical mountain plants to flourish in the heat of the tropics. While it is concerned with recreating nature, the elements for the development have been constructed in such a way as to generate an enhanced ecosystem for the site. The conservatories and the gardens have been designed to be symbiotic, through the interaction of a number of energy and water processes. The conservatory complex is divided into two biomes: the Flower Dome and the Cloud Forest. The Flower Dome will recreate the conditions in Mediterranean springtime – mild but dry days with cool nights. The Cloud Forest will emulate the conditions of tropical mountain regions, areas where the air temperature is relatively mild during the day and slightly chilly at night but with high humidity levels.

In parallel with the design development of the Bay South scheme, NParks had been running a research project with CPG Consultants and Transsolar Energietechnik for several years to determine the required environmental conditions that allow the envisaged plants to grow. As part of this research project, six prototype glasshouses were constructed on the edge of the city to allow study of the behaviour of the plants, and a number of experiments testing alternative environmental conditions were run inside this facility. The research provided data that a peak light level of 45,000 lux was required, benchmarked to the Eden project,[1] and that light levels brighter than this would not add additional benefit to the plants but would increase the building's cooling load; 45,000 lux is about 100 times brighter than would normally be provided in an office environment.

Like plants, the conservatories only need specific frequencies of radiation emitted from the sun to be admitted into the buildings. The facade design is based on a highly selective double-glazed unit that allows approximately 65 per cent of the incident daylight to pass through with only 35 per cent of the solar heat. Low-e coating on the glazing acts as an infrared light reflector filtering unwanted heat from the daylight spectrum. Through the performance simulations of the facade, it became apparent that there were times when more light was reaching the space than was necessary to meet the horticultural requirements. External shading was developed as a response.

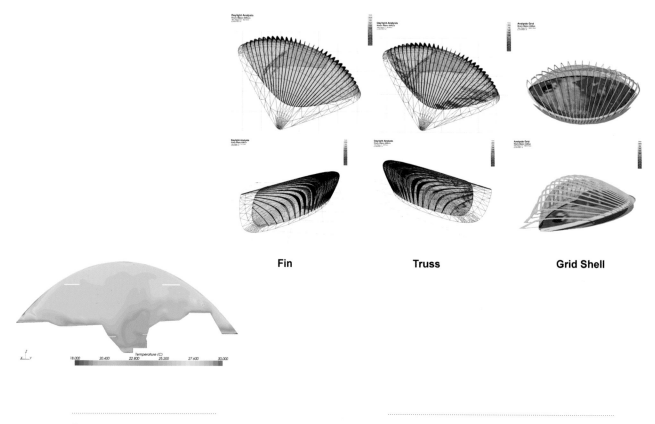

Fin   **Truss**   **Grid Shell**

Computational fluid dynamics (CFD) modelling of hybrid ventilation within the Cloud Forest biome (tropical mountain conditions).

Optimisation of structure for daylighting. Cladding optimisation studies were undertaken by the design team to iteratively form-find the envelope to allow daylight into the building. Fin structure (left), bowstring truss (centre) and grid shell with external beams (right).

Integrated displacement ventilation is to be the primary temperature conditioning method of both biomes, coupled with chilled water being circulated through pipes in the flooring. This displacement system will supply air from diffusers integrated into the vertical surfaces of the planter beds and through displacement diffuser terminals positioned throughout the biome. A central energy centre will provide power, cooling and heat. Within the energy centre a biomass combined heat and power (CHP) plant will generate heat, power and cooling. The intention is for the biomass to be sourced as horticultural residue, currently landfilled and largely from urban street trees pruned in Singapore, in addition to other wood waste streams.

The Supertrees are concrete and steel structures that form a part of the conservatories' conditioning systems as well as the overall site energy management systems. They have a hollow concrete core surrounded by a diaphanous steel-cladding arrangement. At the top of the core is a 'head' that is clad in a membrane material and offers a nearly flat surface, which on a number of the Supertrees houses photovoltaic panels. One of the Supertree clusters near to the central energy centre houses the main boiler flues from the site. The hot and humid exhausted air from some of the building systems is likewise discharged vertically through the 'trunk' of Supertrees forming a cluster adjacent to the conservatories.

Detailed evaluations using a combination of dynamic thermal modelling, computation fluid dynamic and bespoke systems modelling software has proved the performance and determined that the use of these systems makes the provision of cooling to the exhibition spaces within the biomes carbon neutral.

Significant works have been undertaken with respect to water management, largely by Grant Associates and NParks and assisted by Cardno and CPG Consultants. Water is harvested and treated via aquatic landscapes to remediate the received water through a series of interconnected lakes, filter ponds and planting troughs using natural treatment processes.

Approaching the project from first principles allowed the project team and Atelier Ten to look beyond the immediate development horizon to understand the wider context of the project and associated issues to arrive at holistically integrated solutions. Progressive and integrated work methods resulted in a project that seeks to unify both its internal demands and its wider context by forming an enhanced local ecosystem for the development. ⌀

Note
1. The Eden Project, near St Austell in Cornwall, has at its centre a series of large greenhouses formed from ethylene tetrafluoroethylene (ETFE) envelopes designed by Grimshaw Architects. The two main biomes within the facility recreate tropical and Mediterranean conditions. The project opened in 2001.

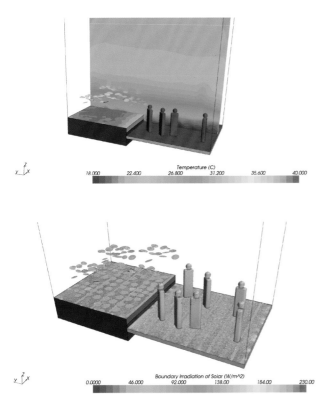

top: Analysis of temperatures around planter beds within the biomes.

above: Detailed modelling for boundary conditions.

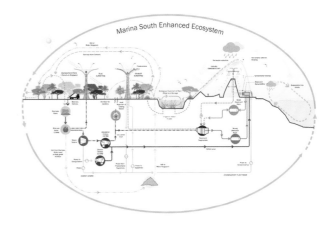

Enhanced ecosystem summarising the differing environmental initiatives incorporated into the project to recreate some of nature's balance.

10 Design/HKU, Indigo Tower, 2011
Wind pressure distribution diagram. The
tower is designed to disperse ventilated air
away from the building. Air flowing through
the residential units is pushed away
from the building to prevent backflow of
potentially contaminated air from entering
other units.

SIGN
UTRALITY

The very term 'sustainable design' implies an aspiration to retain the status quo. What, however, if buildings could have a more proactive effect? Air quality is generally regarded as an environmental problem that has to be tackled by municipal agencies at the urban scale, which architectural design can have little or no impact on. Here **Ted Givens of 10 Design**, a newly established practice in Hong Kong, describes the Indigo Tower, a project undertaken with researchers at Hong Kong University, which explores the way that a building can enhance the wider air quality of its environment through bio-purification.

Newly established Hong Kong architecture studio 10 Design's buildings aim to go beyond mere neutrality and induce positive change. From pollution-eating towers to tornado-proof houses, 10's goal is to develop provocative environmental designs and sustainable strategies that move beyond the range of ordinary design thinking. Innovative conceptual and technical ideas are developed by the studio's sustainability research group and with researchers at Hong Kong University (HKU). 10 uses ecological research to challenge conventions, to explore new ideas and to help adapt and invent new technologies for the built environment.

Urban air quality and pollution are global problems, but these are not normally addressed at building scale. 10 Design looks for ways to combine environmental and architectural quality. The office is currently undertaking research relating to bio-purification, exploring ways that buildings can enhance the air quality in their environment. The research is being tested in a current project, Indigo Tower, a housing tower that purifies air through a combination of passive solar techniques and advanced nanotechnology. The facade of the building is designed to pull dirt, grease and bacteria out of the air. The cleansing reaction is triggered by the use of a nano-coating of titanium dioxide (TiO_2) on the outer skin of the tower. TiO_2 is a strong oxidation agent that is triggered by a

Plan view of CFD wind flow. The twisted form of the Indigo Tower is compared using CFD to a simple rectangular block arrangement. The plan allows for greater wind velocity, greater pressure difference, and less turbulence at the proposed upper-level outdoor balconies.

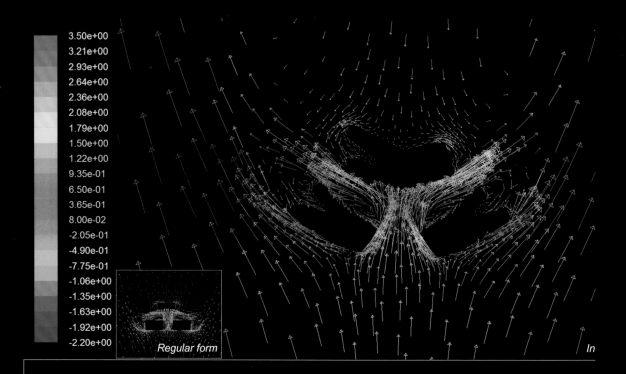

3.50e+00
3.21e+00
2.93e+00
2.64e+00
2.36e+00
2.08e+00
1.79e+00
1.50e+00
1.22e+00
9.35e-01
6.50e-01
3.65e-01
8.00e-02
-2.05e-01
-4.90e-01
-7.75e-01
-1.06e+00
-1.35e+00
-1.63e+00
-1.92e+00
-2.20e+00

Regular form

In

Velocity Vectors Colored By Y Velocity (m/s)

Ma
FLUENT 6.3 (3d,

photocatalytic reaction, which is naturally powered by sunlight, although artificial light will also create the same reaction. Photovoltaic panels mounted on the facade collect and store energy which is used to power a series of ultraviolet (UV) lights to allow the oxidation. A four-layer outer glazing system on the tower keeps the UV light from penetrating the interior of the residential units. At night, the tower becomes a glowing indigo lantern, symbolic of the 24-hour cleansing ritual, in contrast to the yellow haze dominating the city skyline.

The Indigo Tower designs were tested and evaluated for performance using the computational fluid dynamics (CFD) package ANSYS and a CFD solver, ANSYS FLUENT. These tools were used for wind simulation on the tower. ANSYS FLUENT was used for modelling the airflow, turbulence and heat transfer reactions. The building was inserted into a simulation matrix and studied to analyse ways to maximise positive and negative pressure for cross-ventilation, wind velocities across the facade and ways of creating wind shadows for corner balconies. The detailed fluid analysis was done both by the research team at HKU and Laura Rusconi of 10 Design, with constant dialogue between the analysis and the design throughout the project. At many design offices, sun and wind simulation studies are carried out at the end of the design process and therefore

Indigo Tower is a project that underscores how the office views research, design and analysis and weaves these into a fluid and efficient design.

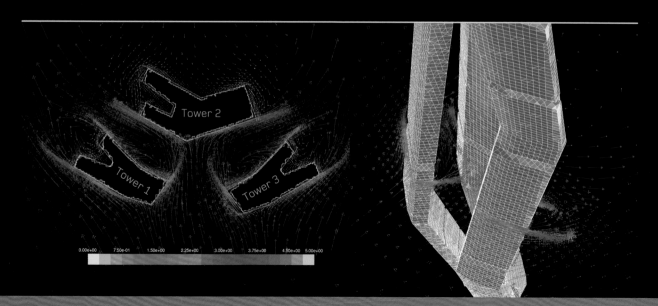

Tower 2

Tower 1

Tower 3

0.00e+00   7.50e-01   1.50e+00   2.25e+00   3.00e+00   3.75e+00   4.50e+00 5.00e+00 *below*: Solar radiation/wind pressure diagram. The splitting of the tower forms and splaying of the two southern forms allows for maximum southern exposure for all units. The twisting of the towers also maximises pressure differences to promote efficient cross-ventilation.

bottom: Air-pressure diagram. Air-pressure and wind-velocity contours are compared at different heights with the regular prism building array using a computational fluid dynamics (CFD) simulation. The unique twisted structure and arrangement of the three towers offers a more effective ventilation path to the approaching wind, promoting ventilation, especially on the leeward side.

opposite top: Night view. Ultraviolet lights located behind the photovoltaic panels on the facade are used to stimulate the continuous air-cleansing chemical reaction. The 240-metre (787.4-foot) tall tower becomes a glowing indigo lantern at night, symbolic of the facade's 24-hour cleansing ritual.

Total Radiation On Building Body
Value Range: 148000.0 - 1296000.0 Wh/m2

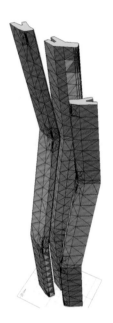

Wh/m2

| 1296000+ |
| 1181200 |
| 1066400 |
| 951600 |
| 836800 |
| 722000 |
| 607200 |
| 492400 |
| 377600 |
| 262800 |
| 148000 |

Body Pressure Distribution

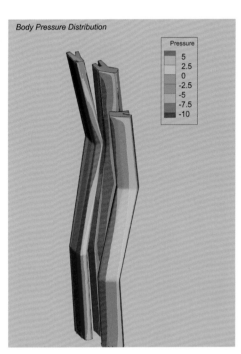

Pressure
| 5 |
| 2.5 |
| 0 |
| -2.5 |
| -5 |
| -7.5 |
| -10 |

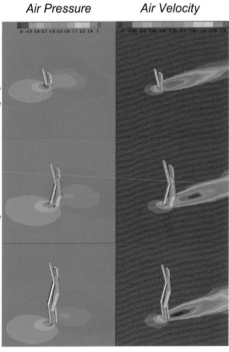

High-zone
220m above ground

Mid-zone
120m above ground

Low-zone
2m above ground

Air Pressure   *Air Velocity*

have little or no design impact other than creating a seductive graphic. At 10, Indigo Tower is a project that underscores how the office views research, design and analysis and weaves these into a fluid and efficient design.

Based on the CFD analysis, the tower's form is split into three vertical elements to increase the amount of surface area, to provide light to the south face of each facade, and to focus and increase wind speed. The increased wind speeds, further focused by the dynamic between the three towers of the building, provide cross-ventilation for every unit in the residential towers and create pockets of positive and negative pressure. The wind turbines are located in zones of maximum pressure. The CFD analysis allowed the design to include balconies located in wind 'shadows' on the facade, to provide comfortable outdoor spaces sheltered from high-speed wind, even at the top of the 80-floor tower. The use of three interwoven vertical towers also helps increase the structural stability of the high-rise and helps to remove excess mass from the neutral axis. Studies have been undertaken to ensure that the backflow air does not flow from one unit into another. Once air has passed through a unit, the ventilated air is pushed away from the building to prevent backflow into another unit. This would help minimise the spread of disease in such a densely populated tower, an issue that was highlighted by the recent SARS outbreaks. Research developed for the cleansing skin of the Indigo Tower is being applied to a confidential 1,000-room resort hotel in southern China, which is at schematic design stage, and will also be utilised on a 200-metre (656-foot) five-star hotel tower outside Shanghai. Construction of both projects will begin in early 2012. The process of research and exploration used in the Indigo Tower illustrates the structure and foundation of 10 Design's work. The office's ultimate goal is to take design beyond the realm of ordinary considerations and, through ecological research, rigorously define new architectural possibilities. ⌂

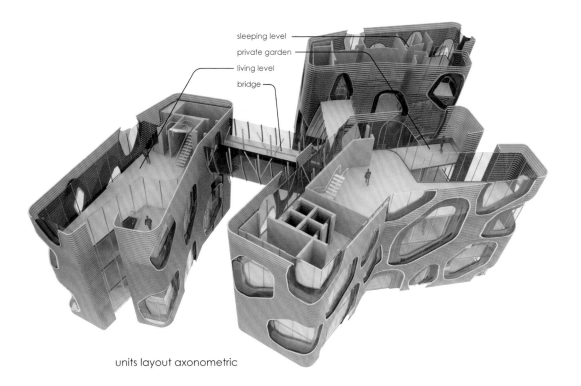

sleeping level —

private garden —

living level —

bridge —

units layout axonometric

Adaptive Building Initiative (ABI), Tessellate™ adaptive facade installation, Simons Center for Geometry and Physics, Stonybrook University, New York, 2010
As Tessellate™ panels move through their range of motion they continuously transition between discrete patterns. Based upon sun position relative to the panels, the overlapping layers can be shifted to maximise or minimise shading effects of off-axis coverage. Shading coverage relative to sun position is determined through ray-traced simulation in order to 'tune' each panel to maximum performance.

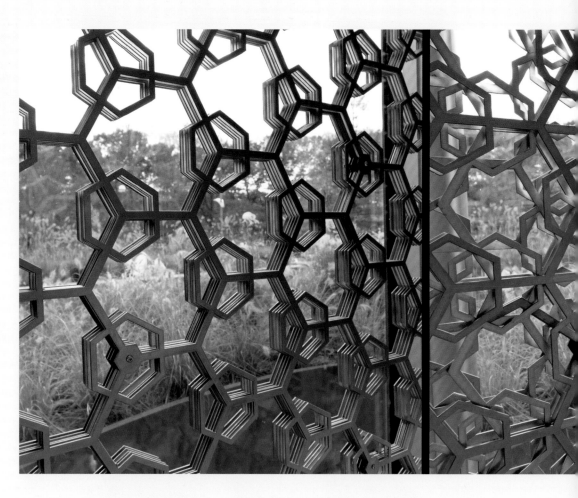

THE ADAPTIVE BUILDING INITIATIVE

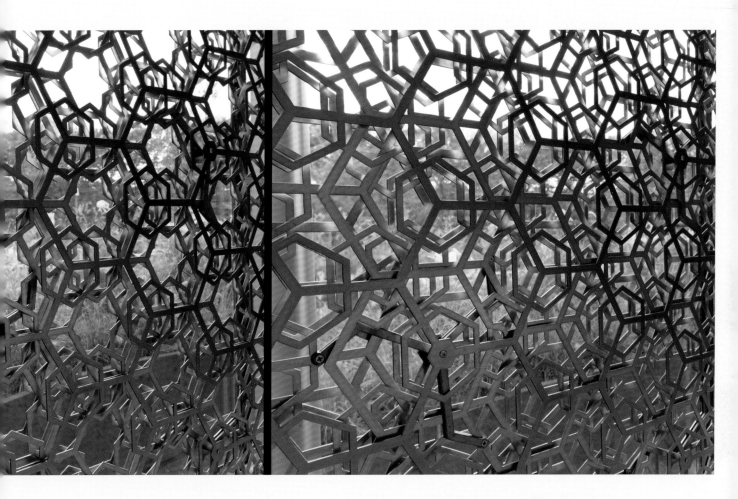

THE FUNCTIONAL AESTHETIC OF ADAPTIVITY

Ziggy Drozdowski, Director of Technology at Hoberman Associates in New York, describes the Adaptive Building Initiative (ABI), a collaboration with engineers Buro Happold that is conceived to catalyse innovation in environmental building performance. The emphasis here is on developing technologies that both architects and engineers can engage with rather than products per se, ensuring that 'the design and the technology layers employed are intertwined into one dynamic system'. This is exemplified by the initiative's development of the Tessellate™ adaptive facade system that both interacts with and helps control incident sunlight.

Ecological research within architectural design practice is often a challenging proposition. On the one hand, the role of the architect is to synthesise a vast array of technical, functional, aesthetic and theoretical concerns into a physical manifestation that embodies the most complete solution for a particular set of circumstances. On the other hand, architects must work within the limits of the building industry and be considerate of technique and technology, and the practical limitations therein. Somewhere between these extremes there lies a solution that advances design thinking through testing certain limits while readily transitioning to buildable architecture.

For the Adaptive Building Initiative (ABI), a collaboration between Hoberman Associates and Buro Happold begun in 2008, occupying this in-between space is paramount to effecting change through design research. In an effort to catalyse innovation in environmental building performance, the impetus for ABI was not to simply create new building products for architects to specify, but to develop enabling technologies that both architects and engineers could engage with in seeking a balance between aesthetics and efficacy. For a building to transcend functionality and truly perform efficiently, it cannot simply be an assemblage of architectural products, but requires that the design and the technology layers employed are intertwined into one dynamic system.

ABI is predicated on creating new technologies derived from novel configurations of classical mechanisms coupled with sophisticated motion control systems. These proprietary mechanical principles enable the manipulation of surfaces in a variety of ways that tend to be of visual interest and can fulfil functional requirements. Through embedded electrical control of this manipulation, behaviours arise that can be systematised, configured, networked and utilised in architectural applications to achieve a functional aesthetic.

The initial thrust of this systems-based technology has been aimed at sun-control strategies, as it is an application that is both critical to building energy efficiency and readily maps to the operation of ABI mechanisms. The appeal of these systems for architects is the ability to embed a needed building function into a designed object, and in effect hide it in plain sight. The right relationship with the designer is imperative, as the customisation and integration of a particular system requires a cohesive team-based design effort. This, in turn, requires that the ABI technology being employed is robust enough to accept a multitude of configurations, and generic enough to allow for a flexible design space that architects can make their own.

The systems developed by Hoberman Associates for ABI are focused around a time-based kinetic behaviour resulting in a combination of visual and functional attributes. Put another way, the work is a combination of something designers demand control over and something they need and have come to expect only cursory control over. This inherent duality to the systems necessitates a two-pronged research effort. The first branch, led by Hoberman Associates, is the core design research, the functional premise and the ingrained flexibility of the design. The second branch, led by Buro Happold, is the functional validation of the system and the degree to which that function can be tuned and implemented within a building to optimise performance.

Each Tessellate™ panel installed at the Simons Center was composed of three or four moving layers of perforated stainless steel that, when retracted, stack to create as little as 20 per cent coverage.

The Tessellate™ adaptive facade system is both an intriguing and functional object in the way it interacts with and helps control incident sunlight.

Performance optimisation is driven by the specific requirements for a particular building and the desired balance between art and ecology that is critical to any modern architectural project. As a first premise for ABI systems, performance is coupled to aesthetics, and the driving aesthetic component is motion. That motion can also be wielded in helping to achieve certain building goals such as blocking sunlight in a particular area at a particular time or allowing increased airflow through a certain barrier. In certain cases, performance may predominate and all aspects of an ABI system (pattern, scale, form factor, number of moving material layers, orientation) will be designed to maximise range of modulation relative to some environmental impulse (light, air, etc). In other cases, design may predominate, but the functional attributes are not completely lost and can still be wielded in the same way, though to a lesser extent.

Even in these cases it has been found through daylight testing of prototypes that, regardless of pattern and scale, having a system that can modulate coverage gradually throughout the day will provide a performance increase over a static element of a similar construction. Ultimately, the major factor in performance is the control scheme to which physical units respond and work together, like an array of analogue pixels that mediate some barrier condition. Each unit on a building is tuned through computer simulation to catalogue its maximum and minimum impact states at all times of the day, and these states are continuously triggered based on building performance objectives. Environmental control schemes are ideally worked out throughout the design process to craft an environmental story, and then validated against models and tuned based on actual data.

Real-Time Research

The core of ABI's technology R&D efforts is the living installation. As a case examination, ABI's Tessellate™ system serves as the most developed example. The basic premise of Tessellate™ is a number of closely stacked perforated screens joined together in a proprietary mechanical configuration that synchronously shift relative to one another. The result is a mechanically efficient modulation of pattern and a change in area coverage. Through deviation in perforation patterning and mechanical detailing, the screen assemblies can vary infinitely with respect to form, size and overall aesthetic.

Through an art commission at Stonybrook University in New York and a prior relationship with A Zahner Co, a high-end artistic and architectural metal fabricator, full-scale prototypes were developed in water-jet-cut stainless steel. The first stage of the final installation has been completed, and ongoing systems-level development is being continued in conjunction with Zahner.

Having built and installed a Tessellate™ system as an architectural element, the real research and development efforts are just getting under way. From an electromechanical systems perspective it is an important test in releasing the technology into the real world to receive feedback. Information such as usage scenarios (autonomy versus manual control), sounds, cleaning and general end-user concerns influence specification and the design of future work. From an environmental perspective, though this installation was not designed to achieve a particular performance objective, it retains the same basic functionality and can be used to correlate real-world data to digital models in the advancement of future simulation efforts. From an architectural design

Tessellate™ panels modulate opacity and can be dynamically controlled or preprogrammed to minimise solar heat gain at certain times of the day while preserving views at other times. Here, Tessellate™ is employed more like a traditional shade where occupants dictate the coverage they desire.

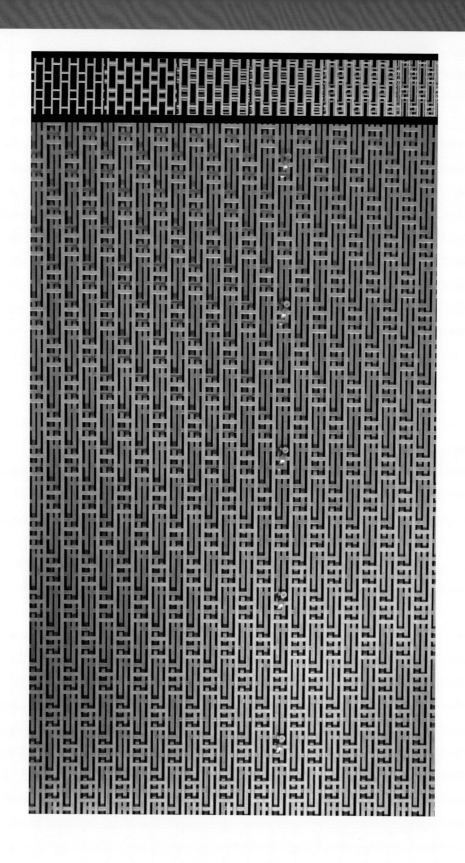

Tessellate™ mock-up composed of two moving layers
The pattern geometry, scale and the number of moving layers of each Tessellate™ panel determine how diffuse the resultant field will be, ultimately impacting the quality of light produced as a functional shade. With this configuration, the area coverage is maximised well before the opening size of the field is unified.

perspective, it stands as something that can be experienced; how it interacts with space and lighting, and how occupiers of that space in turn relate to it.

Tessellate™ is not intended to be a product, but a part of a building. It is an early example of what ABI is attempting to bring to an industry where designers and engineers often work together by defining boundaries. Having taken Tessellate™ to the point of a living installation where technical and aesthetic merits can be evaluated, through the creation of custom design tools ABI allows designers to engage in the aesthetic and shading design aspects of Tessellate™, and bring it directly into their design process, without the need to understand the rigours of the mechanics. It is an experimental workflow that allows ABI to retain certain control over output while empowering designers to push the limits of the technology through their own independent exploration. Clients can advance our collaborations through direct input into our process, effectively blurring the boundaries between design and engineering relative to customisable technology.

Towards Adaptive Buildings

The understanding that buildings have a large ecological impact and are at the forefront of energy concerns is a critical realisation, and the means of engaging with this fact are varied. To ask people to change their behaviour is to expect change through critical inquiry and reflection. But if techniques, tools and systems that are desirable and intriguing while promoting behavioural change are offered, the change may be perceived as more a privilege of advancement than a mandated repentance.

For ABI, facade systems research is about understanding and optimising capability. With a fundamental premise that the capacity for performance is achievable through all proposed systems, the more critical research initiative becomes understanding what designers can implement into their architecture, so that efforts towards ecological systems design actually find their way into the built environment. ᴆ

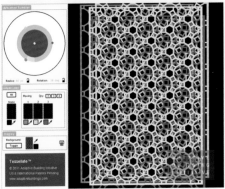

Tessellate™ production at the Zahner fabrication facility, Kansas City, Missouri
top: Each sheet of a panel assembly is individually water-jet cut, allowing for pattern variation with no sacrifice to production time.

Tessellate™ custom pattern design tool
above: The tool is designed so that users input perforation patterns as images, and then adjust and manipulate the mechanism in real time to seek out interesting relationships or more completely shaded states.

ECOLOGY BEYOND BUILDING

PERFORMANCE-BASED CONSUMPTION AND ZERO-ENERGY RESEARCH RAU ARCHITECTS

As the designers of the World Wildlife Fund (WWF) building in Zeist, the Netherlands a CO_2-neutral, self-sufficient office complex, RAU has set the bar for sustainable research and design. Guest-editor **Terri Peters** visited the firm's studio in Amsterdam to talk to principal Thomas Rau. As Peters relates, Rau prefers to put the onus on the dwindling supply of raw materials rather than the immediate problems of energy consumption for which there are solutions within reach. With the emphasis on a more far-reaching approach, he places buildings in a wider context of ecological thinking and systems.

Dutch architect Thomas Rau believes that there is no energy crisis. 'We have solved this,' he explains, 'the new challenge is about raw materials.'[1] His RAU office is known for its building research into energy-saving technologies and concepts for energy-producing buildings. He imagines a future where clients will rent their facades, and design for disassembly and reuse will be commonplace. The office has so far completed CO_2-neutral and nearly zero-energy buildings, and aims to design for energy self-sufficiency and, ideally, energy surplus.

Established in 1992, one of RAU's most well-known projects is the World Wildlife Fund (WWF) building transformation in Zeist, the Netherlands (2006). RAU used ecological research as a way of achieving quality architecture and reducing energy use in this award-winning extension and transformation of a 1950s agricultural factory. The offices were the first CO_2-neutral and (almost entirely) self-sufficient office complex in the Netherlands. To contrast with the original minimalist facades, RAU added a colourfully tiled, three-storey 'hub' in the middle of the existing building. This high-performance hub is the new 'lungs' of the building, revitalising the reception spaces, creating an architectural feature as well as containing significant new sustainable elements. Energy-saving components, such as triple-glazed windows and a grid of wooden exterior louvres to prevent overheating, have been retrofitted into the old building. Solar cells on the roof generate electrical energy and solar thermal collectors are used for heating the water. All walls and ceilings in the new building are plastered with mud, which absorbs moisture and provides insulation. Set into the mud walls is a network of piping that circulates warm or cold water, regulating indoor temperatures. Fitting for a wildlife fund headquarters, birds are encouraged to nest in the roof and there is even a 'bat basement' where bats can use underground spaces as an extension of their natural habitat.

The RAU office philosophy is that clients, developers and designers should take long-term responsibility for their buildings, and that buildings should make a positive contribution to the environment. Rather than discuss ideas of sustainability, which he rejects as a buzzword that means little to his practice, Thomas Rau takes a more ecological, place-based approach. He founded the oneplanetarchitecture institute (OPAi) in 2008, an independent research network focusing on creating sustainable knowledge in collaborative teams relating to architecture, urban design, technology, product supply chains and social structures. The network is concerned with research relating to energy (saving, production, distribution), materials (origin, conversion, life-cycle analysis), organisational development (flow, balance, change, identity) and context analysis (integration into nature, space for nature).

The RAU office philosophy is that clients, developers and designers should take long-term responsibility for their buildings, and that buildings should make a positive contribution to the environment.

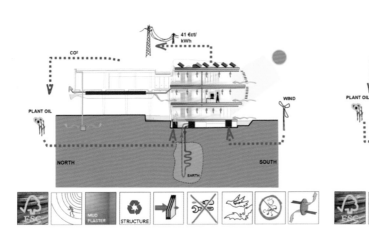
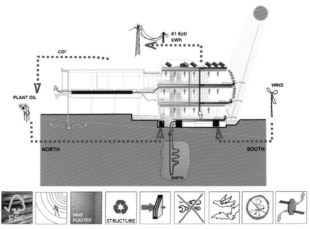

Diagrams of the WWF offices showing the cooling strategies. Cool groundwater is used for cooling the building before flushing toilets. The surplus of warmth in the summer is stored in a water reservoir in the ground and used for heating the building during winter. Likewise, cooling energy is stored underground during winter months and is used for cooling in summer.

Zero-Energy Building Research

Many of RAU and the OPAi's conceptual ideas are being tested in the Woopa project, due for completion at the end of 2011. Woopa is designed to be CO_2 neutral and to produce enough energy to meet its own needs (net zero energy). The project includes social housing, offices, an underground car park and retail. The design team integrated building services knowledge, architectural concepts and urban strategies relating to site access and public transit links from the outset.

Many of Woopa's walls are recycled glass and recycled glass-reinforced concrete, and the architectural design emphasises both passive design techniques and new technological solutions to achieve an efficient building. Natural strategies include ensuring the buildings are correctly orientated to allow optimal daylighting and natural ventilation. Stepped exterior walls and roof overhangs allow some self-shading, which reduces energy consumption for cooling. Technical solutions include an integrated system of sensors that ensures that the building performs in response to where and when people use it, so that empty buildings are not heated and cooled. It is projected that this sensor system alone will save up to 40 per cent of the energy required by a typical building of this size.

Building components were chosen that could reduce time on site and minimise waste. The facade consists of prefabricated sandwich panels that can be assembled quickly and accurately *in situ*, minimising labour and energy in construction. The panels have double-glazed windows with external louvres and a layer of single glazing. These provide insulation against the cold, but also additional sun and heat protection, and users can adjust the louvres themselves. The design of the three layers of glazing allows air to circulate between the panels, allowing the facade to 'breathe' and ensuring that warm air does not become trapped within it.

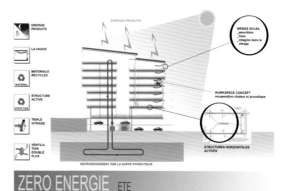

ZERO ENERGIE ETE

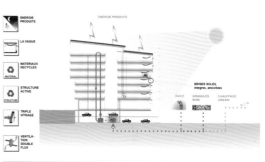

ZERO ENERGIE HIVER

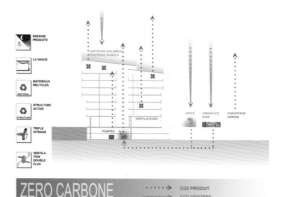

ZERO CARBONE

RAU, Woopa, Lyons, France, 2011
It is projected that once Woopa is in use, a surplus of energy will be produced by this multipurpose building, which can then be fed back into the electricity grid. Calculations at design stage suggest that Woopa will be one of the first large energy-producing buildings in Europe when it is completed in 2011.

Around 2,400 square metres (25,833 square feet) of photovoltaic (PV) cells on the roofs gather and store solar energy, providing electricity to the entire scheme. In order to achieve optimum efficiency from the PV cells, the panels are installed on a double-curved surface at an optimal angle.

The project is designed to be a new benchmark for sustainable development in the region. Many of the strategies are also used in the office's CBW Mitex offices in the woods of Zeist, the Netherlands (2011).

Energy Intranet

The recently completed Christian Huygens College in Eindhoven (2010) is the first CO_2-neutral, plus-energy school in the Netherlands. The project addresses the question of how to design a building that relates to its wider environment. A building's impact and resource use cannot be divorced from its surroundings; it is always a part of its larger ecology. RAU thus collaborated with several industrial and academic research partners to develop an 'energy roof' which allows the college to share and pool resources and create its own energy intranet with the sports hall and housing buildings next to it. Designed with the roofing company Schiebroek, consultants Volantis and researchers from Eindhoven University of Technology, the college roof is a bespoke thermal system based on solar power, which uses an evacuated tube collector with a heat exchanger. The tube collector is covered in synthetic roofing material with an integrated layer of photovoltaic (PV) cells that generate electricity. During peak hours, the system produces more energy than it needs and the surplus energy is stored in an underground water bell storage system. In the winter,

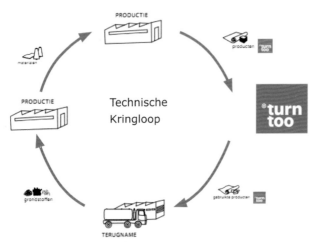

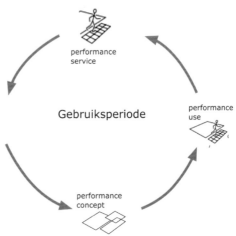

RAU, Christian Huygens College, Eindhoven, The Netherlands, 2010
top: The college is the first CO_2-neutral, plus-energy school in the Netherlands, incorporating both passive and technological energy-efficiency solutions including natural daylighting, ventilation and a high-performance building skin. An innovative 'energy roof' has been designed with academic and industrial partners, saving money and resources.

RAU, Turntoo, 2011
above: Concept diagram. Turntoo promotes innovation from suppliers, reduces waste and landfills, and could lead to cheaper costs for consumers. Because products such as tables, chairs and carpet tiles go back to the manufacturers after a set period of use, the consumer no longer has to be responsible for their disposal. The emphasis is on the producer to create an efficient, easy to disassemble and reuse design. The individuals involved in each part of the supply chain are responsible for their own actions.

this energy can be brought back up to heat the buildings. The development of the energy roof was made possible by a grant from SenterNovem, which calculates a 98.5 per cent CO_2 reduction from both the roof and the PV foil covering it, making the building almost completely CO_2 neutral.

The Future of Performance-Based Consumption

RAU's research and design work focuses on minimising energy use and waste, but Thomas Rau does not believe that energy is the main challenge of ecological design, as with enough money and technical expertise buildings can harness the globe's unlimited supplies of renewable energy, such as solar and wind energy. Instead he sees the real problem for the future as the dwindling supply of raw materials. It is hard to imagine an alternative to raw materials and once they run out, the problem could be impossible to fix.

RAU imagines new ways that buildings and consumers can access performance for their buildings and products without using up raw materials over and over again. For example, in the future clients could rent building facades that have been designed for disassembly, where the cost of maintenance and disposal are the responsibility of the producers. Rau explains: 'Why do we need to own our office furnishings? All we want is a pleasant, inspiring space in which we can do our work efficiently. In any case, what are we supposed to do with

the furnishings at the end of their useful life? As a mature consumer I want to get rid of superfluous property and I don't want to be responsible for the actions of the producers any more.'

The office is testing these ideas of performance-based consumption in Turntoo, a new initiative that aims to create different kinds of relationships with suppliers. RAU approached several producers with the concept, including companies that use cradle-to-cradle principles, and the RAU office interior in Amsterdam is the pilot study. The office buys performance, not materials, using this concept in cooperation with Desso and Interface for flooring, Plugwise for energy monitoring, Philips for lighting and Steelcase for office furniture. Turntoo is a research platform for testing new ideas about consumption and material resources.

Through ecological research – into high-performance building skins, full-scale energy-producing buildings and strategies for products and services – RAU explores ideas of sustainability beyond the building scale. The office considers buildings as part of the ecology of ideas, systems and networks of buildings. Beyond efficiency and energy use, RAU uses these concepts as architectural means of expression, using ecological design as a basis for the creation of inspiring places in which to work, live and learn. ∆

Note
1. Interview with the author, Amsterdam, 19 April 2011.

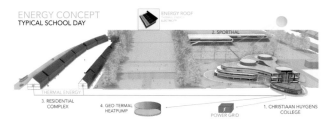 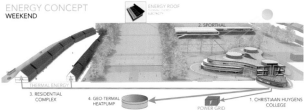

RAU, Christian Huygens College, Eindhoven, The Netherlands, 2010
Diagrams showing the college's energy intranet. The energy concept is centred around the idea of creating an ecology beyond a singular building, allowing sharing of resources. The 'energy roof' and the photovoltaic foil covering it generate enough energy for the college, the housing and the sports hall on the site. The energy is stored and shared among the buildings on the site as needed on demand, with reserves stored underground.

Rachel Armstrong

IS THERE SOMETHING BEYOND 'OUTSIDE OF THE BOX'?

Here, architectural and scientific researcher **Rachel Armstrong** questions whether the definition of 'experimental' green design presented here goes far enough. She urges architects to not dwell on evaluation processes, performance and 'strategies' and to seek a far more radical solution to sustainability, which abandons the current emphasis on industrial technologies and the existing educational and professional frameworks. In its place, she envisions employing biology as a driver for wholly new living materials and systems.

Evan Douglis, Moon Jelly 2, 2011
left and page 133: Douglis' choice of fluid materials produces a holistic yet only partially determined set of architectural tactics that equips the architecture with adaptive potential. Here, two protoplasmic glass agents embody the emergent properties of glass through its ambivalent state between solid and liquid, which generates the context for an architectural matrix that can integrate with the genetic algorithms of digital manufacturing techniques.

Once we fully understand the exact nature of how our world makes us and, indeed how it sometimes kills us, we will be able to make true architectures of ecological connectability. This is our profession's future. Small steps have been made, but much more remains to be done.
— Neil Spiller, 'Plectic Architecture: Towards a Theory of the Post-Digital in Architecture', *Technoetic Arts: A Journal of Speculative Research*, Vol 7, No 2, 2009, pp 95–104

Today's environmental challenges and worldwide population growth demand global fundamental changes in the expectations of architecture in the 21st century and require a radically new kind of system for human development. This is more urgent and avant-garde than the current conversations in this issue of △, which have lost sight of the big picture and have become obsessed with details that do nothing to change a toxic system of architectural practice. The issue simply does not go far enough to address the architectural frameworks, methods, professional bodies and educational practices that have become institutionalised bad habits that serve their industrial masters. It urges us to redefine ecological design research through empirical measurements, to consider new scales of operation, reassess time frames, examine energy efficiency and evaluate building performance. Yet these parameters indicate that the advocates are already trapped within the frameworks they propose to challenge. Inevitably, then, they suggest that less of more of the same kind of approach is warranted. It is not. More of the same, with variations on a common theme, is not a different trajectory than that which already exists. Probing questions must be raised about the current context and expectations of architecture that have become ensnared within an industrial worldview.

In today's commercial climate, the term 'sustainability' petitions for preserving the use of industrial technologies in the promotion of human development, where current practice is wedded to environmental destruction. The success of machines that endorse this perspective is responsible for a century and a half of systematic, environmental rape. This is not recompensed by veiling inert building materials in decorative 'green' tapestries and turning biology into just another part of an architectural machine. The environmentally abusive system itself must be replaced by a radical, more tangible engagement with positive development where buildings are ecologically connected and actively participate in the biosphere. Positive humane development over this coming century actually relies on a totally different approach to architecture that considers environmental 'harm' as completely unacceptable and not just an inevitable part of the process. This does not imply sealing off the environment from human activity by establishing enclaves, biomes and exclusive new utopias such as Masdar, but creating open systems through which architecture orchestrates the co-evolution of populations and their surroundings.

Architects should be taking the lead in proposing alternative frameworks, and this issue highlights interdisciplinary approaches as a means of achieving valuable new knowledge and innovation to address the current malaise in building

Markus Kayser, Solar Sinter, 2011
This solar-powered 3-D fabrication device is guided by digital modelling software to transform sand into glass sculptures.

design. New collaborative practices are vital, but they require the additional shifts in thinking that affect the deepest levels of thought and education. It is not inevitable that practitioners, even from radically different disciplines, will bring the guidance and enlightenment that some of the contributors to this issue of △ seek. Architecture is already well versed in interdisciplinary collaborations; the real issue that needs addressing lies in the homogenising industrial frameworks that constrain the range of possible design outcomes. Moreover, construction methods are constrained by the modern worldview of science on which engineering practices are based, which insists that biology is a machine.

Until these dogmas are challenged, dismantled and new educational programmes are created as a counterpoint to monolithic doctrines, then the same systems of supply, demand, design, manufacturing and implementation will necessarily prevail and architecture will simply be an 'ecological' machine for living in. Michael Lauring even laments the replacement of 'scientific' terms related to ecology with more 'normative' ones that are pictorial and rural, implying a loss of rationality towards environmental issues.[1] In fact, the use of non-empirical ways of engaging design with poetry as a counterpoint to the reductionism, objectification and empiricism of nature can offer a counterpoint to the fundamental assumptions of this epoch. Our biosphere must be considered more than just 'natural capital' and a material resource to be inserted into or consumed by the architectural machine.

Strangling society of energy, making it more expensive and engineering machines to operate more efficiently is not the way to create a positively constructed future. Absolute energy efficiency is desirable within a machine-centred system, but this is not necessarily true for living systems. In fact, energy needs to be freely available and widely exchanged within ecological systems, not just used once and wantonly discarded, as in the case of industrial practices. Energy-efficient processes and careful resource consumption only address the tip of a very large iceberg of systemic issues that have been caused by global industrialisation. Contemporary building practices do more than simply deplete resources and energy. They also, for example, reduce biodiversity, increase waste production and reduce land fertility. A radical reimagining leading to a much more ambitious architectural practice is necessary to change the expectations of what the very act of making a building actually entails.

Product designer Markus Kayser explores new ways of making through his Solar Sinter, a fabrication device that harnesses solar energy to convert sand into glass and bears promising relevance to the exploration of the emergent properties of materials explored by architect Evan Douglis. Combining design, function, computation, aesthetics and an interest in new materials, Douglis engages cutting-edge technology with architectural design in bold new ways. His latest animated exploration, Moon Jelly 2 (2011), suggests a new generation of building tactics by creating a juncture between the old and new that is not imposed on a system, but arises from the fundamental properties of the material itself. His use of the real and apparent slippages between the liquid and solid qualities of glass offers a receptive, material protoplasmic counterpart to the genetic programs of digital manufacturing techniques. The outcome is an approach that encompasses a whole ecology of complementary design techniques from which fundamental architectural agents emerge.

Key to discovering genuinely new thinking processes is the art of drawing, which is a vital process for radical thought experiment. It is ironic that some of the contributors to this issue suggest that drawing is no more than a historical formalism that could be replaced by more efficient tools of documentation and process-orientated, computer-generated graphics. The use of visualisation is arguably the most powerful skill that the architectural profession has to offer an engagement with complex phenomena, and all available methods of design thinking are necessary to explore what constitutes a radical design practice that can challenge existing frameworks of thinking.

Neil Spiller's 10-year Communicating Vessels (2009) project uses drawing to rearticulate the complex, dynamic relationships between seemingly disparate architectural elements encapsulated in this surreal, time-based exploration of a childhood landscape that inhabits an island off the coast of Kent. Within the portfolio of relationships proposed through Spiller's drawings and diagrams, multiple trajectories, layers and transformations are revealed as centres of organising activity between unlikely architectural agents such as the DNA clock obtained from insect amber, a bizarre chicken computer and the idiosyncratic path taken by the flight of a bumble bee. Spiller's point is that architecture must be able to respond to the peculiar and particular circumstances in which it is situated as well as being relevant to the general conditions of its existence, proposing a tactical approach through drawing to achieve this.

Spiller also asserts that practice of the built environment has reached an important point in technology and epistemology where cell biology has become the new cyberspace and nanotechnology, which provides new possibilities in creating ecologically connected architectures that blur the conventional distinction between a building and the landscape. This is rich new territory. Although architecture has a historic engagement with complexity in terms of mathematics and computer science, it has enjoyed little engagement with embodied complex materials due to the lack of available tools, substrates and technologies that can explore these fresh terrains. More experimental media are needed such as the use of film and video as architectural tactics for exploring impacts in an unstable world.

This is the theme of Nic Clear's Unit 15 at the Bartlett School of Architecture, University College London (UCL) which, through the time-based explorations of new media, explores fresh readings of architectural design and construction in increasingly persuasive detail. Dan Tassell's Battersea Project (2011) imagines an architectural scheme where complex 'living' materials such as protocell technologies, which are chemical agents that have some of the properties of living systems but are not considered 'alive', and synthetic biology based techniques[2] set the scene for an ecologically connected self-regenerating architecture to respond to its ambient conditions of use and environmental context. Tassell's project offers something new to the

Dan Tassell, The Battersea Project, Unit 15, Bartlett School of Architecture, University College London, 2011
This self-recycling and reappropriating architectural system makes use of synthetic biology techniques and smart chemical 'protocell' agents to transform London's iconic Battersea Power Station, adapting it to the needs of a constantly changing urban landscape using local resources and harvesting energy from sunlight and chemistry.

architectural experience without destroying what already exists.

Living technologies establish their environmental integrity through sharing common drivers with biology using the 'language' of physics and chemistry. Artist Roger Hiorns exploited these self-organising imperatives in his *Seizure* (2009) installation which transformed a derelict building interior using copper sulphate solution grown *in situ* by harnessing the growth imperative of crystals. These new kinds of living materials provide architecture with an initial point of entry to a whole spectrum of diverse kinds of practice that do not follow a machine paradigm, that create their effects through transformation of matter, working symbiotically with what already exists by acting as organising centres that make and break connections with other hubs of synthetic activity. In this manner, dynamic 'living materials' are proposed to facilitate positive human development through material engagement with local environments by participating in evolvable cycles of chemical exchange.

The outcomes of living systems can reach beyond the expectations of a machine worldview and are compatible with the development of new markets and innovation opportunities. Richard Hyams from Astudio architects is developing an urban scheme through which cities can acquire ecological connectivity by the reskinning of mature concrete and steel frameworks with 'living claddings'. This could lead to a property market where extreme forms of building recycling are a more attractive investment than a newbuild, and would constitute a major shift in building practice that could contribute to our continued survival rather than promoting the destruction of our biosphere. One day this pastoral role conferred by architecture may extend to its human inhabitants. We may even come to think of our buildings as environmental guardians that offer some robust protection against certain unpredictable consequences of climate change and contribute to the regeneration of an urban area, even following a natural disaster. ∆

Notes
1. Michael Lauring, 'From Ecological Houses to Sustainable Cities, Architectural Minds', *The Nordic Journal of Architectural Research*, Vol 22, No 1/2, 2010, p 51.
2. Neil Spiller and Rachel Armstrong, ∆ *Protocell Architecture*, Vol 81, No 2, March/April 2011.

Robert Aish studied industrial design at the Royal College of Art in London and has a PhD in human-computer interaction from the University of Essex. He has developed engineering software with Arup, architectural software with Rucaps, naval architecture software with Intergraph and the GenerativeComponents parametric design software with Bentley. He is a co-founder of the SmartGeometry Group and visiting professor of Design Computation at the School of Architecture at the University of Bath. His role at Autodesk is to converge innovative concepts such as design computation with the mainstream of design and engineering software.

Rachel Armstrong is a co-director of AVATAR (Advanced Virtual and Technological Architectural Research) in Architecture and Synthetic Biology at the Bartlett School of Architecture, University College London (UCL). She is also a Senior TED Fellow and Visiting Research Assistant at the Center for Fundamental Living Technology, Department of Physics and Chemistry, University of Southern Denmark. Her research investigates 'living materials', a new approach to building materials that suggests it is possible for our buildings to share some of the properties of living systems. She was a guest editor of *AD Protocell Architecture* (March/April 2011) and is author of a forthcoming TED book on 'Living Architecture' that will be released on the kindle platform.

Janine Benyus is a biologist, innovation consultant and author of six books, including *Biomimicry: Innovation Inspired by Nature* (William Morrow, 1997), in which she names the emerging discipline that seeks sustainable solutions by emulating nature's designs and processes (for instance, solar cells that mimic leaves). In 1998, she co-founded the Helena, Montana-based Biomimicry Guild with Dr Dayna Baumeister, and in 2006 she co-founded the Biomimicry Institute, a non-profit organisation based in Missoula, Montana.

Peter Busby is the Principal and Managing Director of Perkins+Will's Vancouver office. He directs more than 100 employees working on projects internationally and provides sustainable

design leadership to the firm's 23 offices worldwide. He is a founder of the Canada Green Building Council.

Chip Crawford is a landscape architect and the Practice Director of the HOK Planning Group. In addition to being a Fellow of the American Society of Landscape Architects, he serves on HOK's Board of Directors and Design Board, as well as on the ASLA CEO Roundtable. He recently served as President-Elect of the Board of the Landscape Architecture Foundation.

Meredith Davey is a chartered engineer and chartered environmentalist, with degrees in physics and design art. He joined Atelier Ten in 2005 and leads the UK Environmental Consultancy team. He provides engineering, high-performance design and sustainability consultancy throughout the world and has worked on a number of landmark international projects during his career.

Christian Derix has been head of Aedas' Computational Design and Research group since 2004. The group develops computational models for design processes in architecture with an emphasis on space planning and human occupation. He studied architecture and computational design and has taught and researched the subject at the University of East London, University College London, Politecnico di Milano and the Technical University Vienna.

Michael Driedger is a sustainability building advisor at Perkins+Will and a LEED® Canada accredited professional with 15 years of experience working in the construction trades, architecture and research. His diverse work experience has helped develop his talents in project management, LEED coordination, research and building carbon emissions analysis.

Ziggy Drozdowski has been with Hoberman Associates since 2004 and currently holds the position of Director of Technology. He has also been working to help shape the Adaptive Building Initiative through project work and R&D efforts since its inception in 2008. His work ranges from computational design and modelling to motion control system

specification and implementation. He received his bachelor's degree in engineering from the Cooper Union, specialising in electrical engineering and acoustics.

Irene Gallou is an environmental design analyst at Foster + Partners. Her role involves assessing the impact of buildings and open spaces on the environment. She studied architecture at the University of Rome, before completing a Masters in Energy and Environmental Studies at the Architectural Association (AA) in London.

Ted Givens is a design partner at the newly formed 10 Design in Hong Kong. He has recently won seven out of eight design competitions in Asia and is dedicated to sustainable research and design.

Fabienne Goosens graduated as a chemical engineer at Delft University of Technology in 2010. She has a strong drive to analyse complex problems related to sustainability, exploring the cultural, technological and environmental dimensions to sustainability. She is a freelance researcher with 2012Architecten and currently works as a process engineer at Attero supporting the development of waste management technologies of the future.

Jan Jongert graduated as an architect at the Academy of Architecture Rotterdam in 2003. As co-founder of 2012Architecten in Rotterdam he designs interiors and buildings and develops strategies to facilitate the transition to a sustainable society. He specialises in the behaviour of flows in the interior, industrial and urban environment. He currently leads a research group, INSIDE flows, at the new mastercourse for interior architecture at the Royal Academy in the Hague.

Kasper Guldager Jørgensen is Director of GXN, cand.arch.maa, and associate partner at 3XN. He also teaches at the Royal Danish Academy of Fine Arts School of Architecture, and is a board member of the Danish Society of Material Technology. He has written numerous articles and books, and is also an invited speaker at many architectural and technical universities internationally.

Abdulmajid Karanouh is an architect, with an MSc in computational design and facade engineering. An associate at Aedas London, he was lead designer on the Al Bahr Towers in Abu Dhabi and specialises in systems design and integration. His interest in performance-oriented and responsive design has led to the development of an approach that includes mathematical and engineering integration from concept design to realisation. Previous experience includes hi-tech facade engineering with Folcrá where he developed solutions for architects including Santiago Calatrava and Richard Rogers. He is a guest speaker at universities and seminars in the US, UK and Middle East, and has written papers addressing the integration of technology in building design.

Azam Khan is Head of the Environment & Ergonomics Research Group at Autodesk where he has been exploring modelling and simulation including physics-based generative design, airflow and occupant flow in an architectural context, and simulation visualisation and validation based on real-time sensor networks. In 2009 he founded SimAUD to foster cross-pollination between the simulation and architectural research communities.

Judit Kimpian is Head of Sustainability and Advanced Modelling at Aedas, where she develops designs that take advantage of computational techniques to maximise sustainable value. Her approach to visualising and manipulating the spatial, environmental and financial relationships has provided the basis for her collaboration with RIBA and CIBSE to develop the national carbon monitor scheme CarbonBuzz.

Mary Ann Lazarus is the firm-wide Sustainable Design Director at HOK. With more than 30 years' architectural experience with HOK, she drives the implementation of sustainable strategies in all the company's work. She co-authored *The HOK Guidebook to Sustainable Design* (John Wiley & Sons, 2005), and helped spearhead the unique alliance between HOK and the Biomimicry Group to bring biomimicry to the built environment.

Laura Lesniewski is an architect at BNIM Architects and led the design team on the Omega Center for Sustainable Living, the first project in the world to achieve 'Living' status in the Living Building Challenge and LEED Platinum. She is co-author (with Steve McDowell) of *Flow: The Making of the Omega Center for Sustainable Living* (ORO Editions, 2010), which chronicles the design and construction of this net-zero project.

Andrew Marsh is an architect, building scientist and software author. He is Senior Principal Engineer at Autodesk, working on the relationship between building information modelling (BIM) and building performance analysis. He was previously co-founder and head of development at Square One Research where he worked on performance-driven building projects and authored a range of architectural science and analytical design software tools, including Ecotect.

Josh Mason is a Senior Designer in Aedas' Advanced Modelling Group, focusing on complex geometry projects and incorporating environmental and engineering principles into parametric design models. He studied mechanical and civil engineering at Columbia University, New York, and emergent technology and design at the Architectural Association in London.

Nels Nelson graduated as an urban environmental manager from Wageningen University and Research Centre in the Netherlands in 2010. He is challenged by contemporary urbanisation versus the legacy of 20th-century infrastructure.

Katsumi Niwa is a senior energy and environmental consultant at Nikken Sekkei Research Institute (NSRI). He joined Nikken's M&E Engineering Division in 1989 after earning a Master of Engineering degree from Kobe University, and joined NSRI in 2009. He is a professional engineer (HVAC) and senior registered architect of Japan, and a member of a number of organisations including the Japan Institute of Architects and the Society of Heating, Air-Conditioning and Sanitary Engineers of Japan. He is also co-author of the *Handbook of Air-Conditioning and Sanitary Engineering*, and teaches mechanical engineering design to graduates and undergraduates at university level.

Max Richter is an architect at Perkins+Will bringing experience in sustainable design on a variety of transportation, infrastructure and government projects. He has particular interest in using daylight in creative ways to achieve beautiful spaces and energy-efficient buildings.

Hugh Whitehead is Head of the Specialist Modelling Group at Foster + Partners. He leads a team of analysts that carry out research and development, the results of which are fed into every stage of the design process. He graduated from the University of Liverpool in 1973 where he was awarded a first class honours degree for research on optimisation applied in an architectural context.

Tomohiko Yamanashi is Chief Architect and Design Section Principal of the Architectural Design Department at Nikken Sekkei. He has a Master of Urban Design degree from the University of Tokyo, which he acquired in 1986. The same year he joined Nikken as an assistant architect. He has won numerous awards, his latest being MIPIM Asia's Special Jury Award in 2009 for Mokuzai Kaikan. He is a member of the Japan Institute of Architects and the Architectural Institute of Japan, and also teaches architectural design to graduates and undergraduates at university level.

Simos Yannas is the Director of the Environment & Energy Studies Programme at the Architectural Association (AA) School of Architecture in London and academic coordinator of the school's PhD programme. He is also a Sir Isaac Newton Design Fellow in Architecture at the University of Cambridge. His latest book is *Lessons from Vernacular Architecture* (Earthscan, 2011). His earlier *Roof Cooling Techniques: A Design Handbook* (Earthscan, 2005), co-authored with Evyatar Erell and Jose Luis Molina, was shortlisted for the RIBA International Book Award for Architecture.

INDIVIDUAL BACKLIST ISSUES OF △ ARE AVAILABLE FOR PURCHASE AT £22.99 / US$45

TO ORDER AND SUBSCRIBE SEE BELOW

What is Architectural Design?

Founded in 1930, *Architectural Design* (△) is an influential and prestigious publication. It combines the currency and topicality of a newsstand journal with the rigour and production qualities of a book. With an almost unrivalled reputation worldwide, it is consistently at the forefront of cultural thought and design.

Each title of △ is edited by an invited guest-editor, who is an international expert in the field. Renowned for being at the leading edge of design and new technologies, △ also covers themes as diverse as: architectural history, the environment, interior design, landscape architecture and urban design.

Provocative and inspirational, △ inspires theoretical, creative and technological advances. It questions the outcome of technical innovations as well as the far-reaching social, cultural and environmental challenges that present themselves today.

For further information on △, subscriptions and purchasing single issues see: www.architectural-design-magazine.com

How to Subscribe

With 6 issues a year, you can subscribe to △ (either print or online), or buy titles individually.

Subscribe today to receive 6 issues delivered direct to your door!

INSTITUTIONAL SUBSCRIPTION
£230 / US$431 combined
print & online

INSTITUTIONAL SUBSCRIPTION
£200 / US$375 print or online

PERSONAL RATE SUBSCRIPTION
£120 / US$189 print only

STUDENT RATE SUBSCRIPTION
£75 / US$117 print only

To subscribe:
Tel: +44 (0) 1243 843272
Email: cs-journals@wiley.com

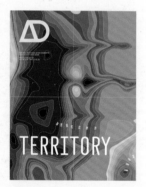

Volume 80 No 3
ISBN 978 0470 721650

Volume 80 No 4
ISBN 978 0470 742273

Volume 80 No 5
ISBN 978 0470 744987

Volume 80 No 6
ISBN 978 0470 746622

Volume 81 No 1
ISBN 978 04707 47209

Volume 81 No 2
ISBN 978 0470 748282

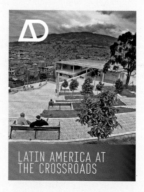

Volume 81 No 3
ISBN 978 0470 664926

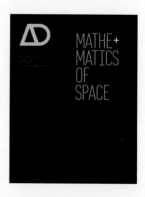

Volume 81 No 4
ISBN 978 0470 686806